$1.00/day Overdue Fine

THE GEIGER COUNTER

RAISED BY WOLVES
& OTHER STORIES

THE GEIGER COUNTER

RAISED BY WOLVES
& OTHER STORIES

MATT GEIGER

HENSCHELHAUS PUBLISHING, INC.
MILWAUKEE, WISCONSIN

Published by
HenschelHAUS Publishing, Inc.
www.henschelHAUSbooks.com

ISBN: 978159598-496-8
E-ISBN: 978159598-497-5
LCCN: 2016948171

Printed in the United States of America

For Hadley

Table of Contents

PREFACE

The following stories originally appeared, in somewhat different form, in the *Middleton Times-Tribune*, the *News-Sickle-Arrow*, the *Mount Horeb Mail*, and other *News Publishing, Co.* publications.

THE MURDERER

I remember my dad, holding a rifle and rocking in an old wooden chair as he peered out of the second-story bedroom window. The farm where we lived was miles from the nearest streetlight, so he was primarily looking into a reflective glass void in which the ghost of a middle-aged man in a flannel shirt sat in a chair, cradling a gun and occasionally sipping whiskey.

There was a murderer on the loose, and my dad was going to shoot him, I thought.

Living in a small town on the New England coast, excitement of this variety was in short supply. My companions were meditative cows, emotionally distant barnyard cats, and a pet dog who, if let loose, would literally run in a straight line until he died, was caught and returned, or circumnavigated the earth and ended up back at his food dish.

The most homicidal thing I'd ever seen up until that day was the zip-line I tried to build between two tall maple trees in a nearby wood. That and my dad when I returned home from using the zip-line, asking if someone could help me search for all the missing skin that had been flayed from my hand.

But this was a real, human murderer. Two law enforcement agents in gray suits had knocked on our door that morning and explained the situation to my parents.

From my listening spot around the corner, I had to cobble together the information from various conversational tidbits. But the basics were clear. A maniac had escaped custody, and his pursuers' chase had led them to our front door.

Surrounded by a thousand sprawling acres of land and dozens of old, vaguely English agricultural buildings, this was an escaped convict's dream come true. There were moss-covered stone walls behind which to duck. Musty hay lofts in which to sleep. Cows to milk if he got thirsty, and horses on which to gallop away to freedom if he was not too busy stabbing us all to death in our beds.

It was the greatest event of my young life. As night closed in around us, it blotted out the equipment and buildings in the barnyard, replacing them, in my mind's eye at least, with this crazed and violent man. Every lowing of a cow meant he was tip-toeing through the muck. Every rustle of the leaves was his weight shaking the tree he scaled to leap onto our roof. Every silence was him holding his breath as he plotted something extraordinarily bloody.

I had been planning a career in either baseball or masked vigilantism for years, and it appeared fate had made the final decision for me. Now was the time to reveal myself as a top-flight crime fighter.

I played the situation over and over in my head. Each one ended in the same way, with me the hero. Like most of my life goals then and now, the story followed the same narrative arc. I would avoid putting myself in any real danger, but chance would eventually deliver the criminal to me in some way.

Perhaps I could stick my leg out around a corner as FBI agents chased him by, tripping him so they could cuff him and haul him away. Or maybe he would fall asleep and I could creep out of the food pantry and hit him over the head with a frying pan. Or maybe he would simply crumple of exhaustion at my feet just before the police arrived.

However it went down, they would find me with my arms crossed and one foot resting atop the fallen villain.

Was this something for which I should put on my Batman costume? No, that would be ridiculous.

I would dress as Zorro. Slashing a "Z" into this man's torso would be a fitting way to cap my victory over evil.

Wait, no. I would be Inigo Montoya from *The Princess Bride*. The FBI agents hadn't mentioned anything about this man having six fingers, which Montoya's nemesis did. But they hadn't said anything about him not having six fingers, either. In fact, they had been surprisingly silent about how many digits he had. Probably because he had six and they didn't want to sound politically incorrect by bringing it up, I surmised.

In hindsight, my dad showed commendable restraint by not shooting me that evening, as I repeatedly sprang out from behind him and yelled: "Hello! My name is Inigo Montoya. You killed my father. Prepare to die!"

He just smiled, sighed, and turned his attention back to the window.

In all my excitement, I don't remember feeling any actual fear. My dad was there, after all, and he would make sure any harm that befell me would be the wholesome, skinned-knee variety, not the terrifying, hacked-to-bits-with-a-cleaver type.

It is in the absence of fear that we are all at our best. Being afraid, after all, is the most toxic emotional state. It's why the Internet is such a weird place—because that's where everyone goes to express their most hyperbolic terror. Republicans are scared of the government. Democrats are scared of Republicans. The old are scared of the young, and so on.

When afraid, we cower and lose sight of all that is good. But when your dad is calmly guarding your home from an escaped lunatic, you can put on your best cowl or cape, let your imagination go wild, and really make the most of the situation.

I sometimes hear other parents pointing out all there is to fear in the world. "Stay away from strangers, animals, television, cell phones and above all, wheat," they advise. "Just generally remember that everything on earth is dangerous."

My message to my daughter is a little different, at least during these early years. There are two potential scenarios she will encounter until she's old enough to venture off on her own.

The first is that everything is fine. The second, like that evening with the murderer on the loose, is that everything is not fine, but she doesn't need to worry or be afraid because I'm here to make sure everything is okay.

For the first year of her life, my daughter was essentially a backpack. An inanimate object. The key to successful parenting was the same as the key to successful backpack ownership: If you ever set it down, make sure you pick it up again before you leave.

But people, most of them women, marveled at me when they saw me doing it.

"Look at that man," their eyes said. "He's carrying something that weighs 20 pounds and he's buying a loaf of bread. Wow!"

Their adoration made me wonder if their husbands, when sent to the grocery store to fetch diapers, often came home without the baby but with a pet giraffe or a giant new tattoo. Or maybe they made a habit of forgetting their infants in the organic produce section, left with only a smug sense of culinary superiority to keep them company.

These people look at me as they would a chimpanzee wearing glasses or a dog riding a skateboard. Impressed merely by the fact that I'm doing something, but the bar set so low they don't even bother to check if I'm doing it well.

But keeping your kid alive comes naturally, whether that means not forgetting her at the supermarket or arming yourself and fighting off a violent escaped convict.

And he never did kill my family, by the way. The police found him a few days later, shivering and afraid, in a barn a few miles down the road. At the time, I thought the important thing was that my dad had kept him away.

Today, I know I was wrong. My dad didn't sit there all night to keep the murderer away. He was there to keep out the fear. To fend off the most useless of emotions.

And it worked, of course. Because sometimes things are fine, and sometimes monsters lurk in the shadows. And while you can't actually protect your kids from every bump and bruise, you can protect them from fear.

Because when you are very young, you should be beyond fear's reach. And when it tries to get in, it's good to know there is someone there, standing guard, looking into the darkness and keeping it at bay.

MY MONKEY

"Hello? Yes, this is Mr. Geiger. I would like to buy a monkey, et cetera, et cetera."

I stood in the archway of our walk-in food pantry, eyeing a plastic, five-gallon vat of honey and a shining, dented metal tub of flour. A few feet from our kitchen door, two goats were munching on hay, working their jaws in an eternal circular motion as they looked in at me like I was insane.

I had somehow become hopelessly entangled in the long, spiraling black cord that linked the heavy telephone receiver to the wall.

I referred to myself as "Mr." so the man on the other end of the phone would think I was an adult, and that I therefore possessed the authority to purchase a primate.

The "et cetera" bit at the end was freelancing; the repetition of words I had only heard adults say, which I hoped would make me sound more serious and profound.

"I would like it mailed to my house," I continued. "We live on the farm on 1A, and we have lots of trees here for him."

There was an uncertain pause, so I decided to sweeten the pot with a word I frequently heard my father say when he was buying things.

"MasterCard."

"Son," said the man on the other end of the phone. "How old are you?"

Old enough, I knew, to want a pet monkey. That was what mattered.

"There are no refunds, I hope?" I enquired, strategically dodging his question with one of my own.

This was a key component of my plan. If there were no refunds, my parents would have to keep the monkey. The only other option would be to simply throw their money away, which felt unlikely.

I would be punished severely for making a long-distance call to Florida, surely. I might even get grounded.

But I would have a monkey to play with, and our shenanigans would make leaving the house unnecessary.

"Please send him to Ipswich, Massachusetts. Master-Card. Et cetera," I added for good measure. "And I would prefer a cool monkey. Not a weird one. If you have one that knows how to play baseball, send him."

The monkey vendor, his voice tinny as it traveled to me all the way from Florida, was unimpressed. He gave many reasons why he was hesitant to mail me a monkey. He couldn't ship monkeys across state lines. He made it a habit never to sell violent, semi-wild animals to small children. Plus, that being Florida, he had been working diligently to cut down on the amount of business he did with the unhinged.

In the end, I failed to obtain my monkey. To make matters worse, my dad did not fail to obtain a conspicuously high long-distance charge on his next phone bill.

I was grounded, and I didn't even have a furry little man, clad in a diaper and a bowler hat, to help pass the time.

Years later, my philosophy professor got to sit down for a chat with a great ape that spoke sign language. She was an ethicist (the professor, not the gorilla), and the university had arranged for her to ask the hulking black mass of a creature a list of questions about the nature of truth, right and wrong, and God.

My teacher, whose red hair was prone to anarchy and apparently wore nice shoes that day, found the gorilla's answers lacking.

"It was a complete waste of time," she moaned. "She just kept asking about my shoes. I asked her if she believed in God, and she replied with: 'Please may I touch your red foot hats?'"

The fact that I had never obtained my own personal primate still stung, even all those years later. Plus, my teacher had committed the worst sin of all. Worse than murder. Worse even than arguing about politics on social media.

She had done something amazing, yet completely failed to appreciate it.

"It was dumb," she complained. "She wouldn't answer any of my questions about Aristotle."

"Yeah," I countered. "But you got to have a conversation. With a gorilla."

Put me in the room with a great ape that has mastered the art of language, and I will happily chat for days—months even—about shoes, gloves, the weather, or whatever else happens to catch my new friend's fancy.

In fact, if I had to choose between sitting down for a long talk with Jean Paul Sartre about existentialism or a conversation with a gorilla about footwear, I'd take the gorilla every time.

But some people struggle to see the spectacular, even when it is right in front of them. It is an affliction I would not wish upon my greatest enemy.

After graduating from college, I took my degree in philosophy and marched into a large zoo's human resources department.

"I would be willing to talk to you about metaphysics for money," I offered. "Or, if you prefer, I would also be willing to shovel animal manure."

They were in need of the latter, so I spent the next year caring for camels and draft horses, just a few minutes' stroll from the great ape house.

When my daughter was a few months old, I took her to yet another zoo. I enjoyed fatherhood for many reasons, perhaps chief among them being the fact that my daughter provided many of the qualities I had been longing for when I tried to buy a monkey from a befuddled Florida man thirty years before.

She wore a diaper, climbed all over the house, and I was even able to procure a little bowler hat for her.

Standing a few feet from a family of orangutans, I whispered to her: "Look at those big, shaggy, red apes. Aren't they amazing!?"

"Ohh..." she exclaimed.

When I looked down, I noticed she wasn't even looking at the animals. I don't think her eyesight went that far yet.

Instead, she was staring at a metal railing, a mere foot from her face, on which a little sign offered a few mundane words about the beasts.

"No, you silly little monkey, that's not the amazing thing," I said. "That's just a steel bar with a sign on it. The amazing thing is over there."

It was probably the first time my daughter, who wouldn't even say her first word for another several months, gently corrected my folly.

She kept staring at the railing, which was painted a dull rust color. Then she smiled.

That's when I realized a simple piece of steel, and certainly a sign, are some of the most spectacular things I'll ever encounter. Humankind's ability to mine ore from the earth and smelt it into swords, armor, buildings and eventually cars and space ships, is one of the most important advancements in our history as a species.

And a few simple words on a sign at the zoo represent something even more remarkable: Language, which is certainly as close to magic as we will ever really come in this world, should be marveled at whenever the opportunity arises. What is casting a "spell," after all, but the spelling out of powerful words.

It's an important lesson, et cetera, et cetera.

THE NUTCRACKER

I used to own a lot of nutcrackers. Little, brashly painted wooden men who looked like Russian princes in rigor mortis.

They were, I thought at the time, the worst action figures ever created.

My parents were friends with some of the people who helped run a ballet company in New England. We would sojourn at their home each year, where their two abnormally tall daughters would tower over me as we sat around the table, munching on Maine lobster and chatting about things that did not interest me in the slightest.

Things were different in their house. At our home, furniture was for sitting. Here, it was for looking at and talking about.

I once tried to plop down on an object that looked pretty unambiguously like a chair. Four wooden legs, a plush seat, and a straight back all indicated to me it was a place where weary or, in my case, bored people could go for respite.

The thing I noticed first was the horror in the behemoth young girls' eyes.

Was I, I wondered as my backside touched the seat, about to sit on a whoopee cushion? Possibly a nail?

"Matthew!" shrieked Jane, the family's matriarch, as I settled in, though no flatulence had sounded and I had felt no sharp pain. "That chair is an antique!"

They never looked at me the same again. Relegated to a remedial bench of no particular importance, I was looked down upon as a dangerous little plebian who was liable to sit on any expensive object you left lying around the house.

It ate away at my confidence. If their chairs weren't for sitting, perhaps other household items were not for their presumed purposes either. I hesitated at the dinner table, making sure other diners were using their forks to spear morsels of food. Doorknobs, tables, even shoes stacked by the door became objects of trepidation. Did they also have other applications, unknown to my dull mind?

"Over there is the swimming pool where we cook our food," they'd say. "And that's the bathroom where we play ping-pong."

All I really wanted on these journeys was to see a bull moose. In movies and on television, these giant creatures roamed woods, backyards and village streets in great numbers.

Instead, all I ever found in Maine were people with flowing dresses, clanky metal bracelets, big hoop earrings, floral perfumes, dark glasses of expensive wine and endless trays of hors d'oeuvres I could barely identify as food.

"What are those?" I once asked a male ballet dancer at a gathering.

"Those are sandwiches, Matt," he replied. "Heh, heh, Matt doesn't know what sandwiches are."

At my house, sandwiches were made of meat and cheese or peanut butter and jelly, wedged between two slices of bread. The thing on the plate in front of me contained none of those elements.

I overheard the ballet guy talking with a ring of friends later that evening, telling them about the massive moose he almost hit with his car on the way to a performance one night.

"You have got," I thought to myself, "to be kidding me."

We would all go to see the company's production of *The Nutcracker* during the holidays. It was where I learned that, while sitting in chairs was a grievous faux pas, it was perfectly acceptable to jump and twirl around on a stage, wearing clown make-up and tights that simultaneously shimmered and gelded.

I had nothing in common with anyone. Even worse, I was unsure if objects were as they seemed.

After the performance one night, Jane said we would all be going out to a fancy restaurant together. We could all pile into their car, she said.

"Right," I muttered. "A car. For riding in, right?"

At a loss for something to say over the meal, I looked over at a resplendent red, black and gold nutcracker sitting with a pile of other ballet-related trinkets.

"That's pretty interesting," I commented, secretly yearning for someone with whom I could talk about Batman or baseball.

It's one of those odd cruelties to which I've been submitted in my life. The fact that my parents went instantly and completely deaf on the hundreds of occasions I asked for a bazooka as a child. Yet this one small comment was heard by everyone in the restaurant, and they all, apparently, made a note of it.

So every Christmas, year after year, I received ornately wrapped packages from my parents' ballet friends.

Inside was always a baroque, hand-carved and hand-painted nutcracker.

"Oh, boy," I said the first time I opened one, lying through my teeth the way adults had taught me to do in most public situations. "This is great."

Everything in their world was upside down, so I felt like perhaps I wasn't being dishonest. Maybe here, "great" meant terribly disappointing.

"Well," I said with manufactured enthusiasm. "Let's try it out."

As I reached for a bowl of nuts, I saw horror in everyone's eyes.

"Matthew!" Jane called out with a giggle. "That's decorative. It's not for cracking nuts."

IN THE GRAVEYARD

At the center of an ancient graveyard, in a mossy stone shrine, sits a little statue believed to hold magical powers.

It is a small figurine, painted thick with unapologetically bright slabs of blue and orange. Sitting in a hut lined with church pews and votive candles featuring saints with fashion sense akin to that of a Mexican wrestler, it is the Virgin Mary nursing her infant deity.

She is called *Nuestra Seniora de la Leche y Buen Parto*. It sounds exotic in Spanish, but vaguely like a badly translated Chinese menu offering when morphed into English: "Lady of the Milk and Happy Delivery."

This old Catholic mission is a place of balmy beauty, with palm fronds littering a moss-covered scenery. The grass is a canvas on which a pristine bay has been painted.

It also smells distinctly of death, or at least rotten eggs, because that part of Florida is oozing with sulfur-water. There is nothing quite as unsettling as standing at dusk in a cemetery that smells so specifically like decay.

Today the place is a tourist attraction, where I once worked as a historian and, because that's not a real job, a groundskeeper.

But it all began long ago. On the night of August 20, 1565, a group of Spanish sailors, convinced they were about to die in a terrible storm, spent the entire night confessing their sins to the ship's chaplain. Their last ditch effort to get into heaven was in vain, however, as the weather eventually cleared.

On September 6, they arrived in what is now Florida, very much alive and ready to sin anew.

As a result of the things that happened between their arrival and mine, it was one of those sites that could never decide if it was tragic or not. It was mostly a graveyard, filled with victims of various plagues and fevers that used to descend upon mankind in a dazzling spectrum of colors. It also had a glistening gift shop full of Catholic baubles and brochures directing you to the nearest shopping mall, as well as a nearby warehouse holding wholesale church supplies.

It was a few miles down the road from Ponce De Leon's legendary Fountain of Youth, where tourists from around the world journeyed to pinch their noses and make disappointed faces when they realized the water had a perfume of old socks and a bouquet of August sewer grate.

It was, according to the thousands of Catholics from across the world who traveled there each year, the birthplace of their faith in North America. It began when a short, bearded man named Don Pedro Menendez was freed from prison and sent west to claim lands for his Spanish queen.

The old mission was also a place of death for the French Protestants who showed up a few days earlier but were laid to rest by Floridian weather and Spanish steel.

Likewise, the Timucua Indians, who records show lived in a nice village on that exact spot in 1565, are nowhere to be found today.

While a nearby church gave ethereal ceremonies marking birth, love and death, I swept up dust from the floor of a warehouse in which towering stacks of boxes of sacramental wine threatened to come crashing down with biblical, purple panache.

The head groundskeeper—who was only in charge by default, as he was the only groundskeeper except me—was a beach bum. He was like Jimmy Buffett but with no money. With sun-bleached stubble that insinuated homelessness rather than the carefree life of a pirate.

Joe did own a boat. I believe "dingy" is the technical term. In it he came and went in the mercurial manner of a semi-domesticated cat.

He was thin the way starving people are thin, not in the casual manner of first world dieters. His veins lay like lines of thick cable just below orange skin. His hair had once tried to be either blond or gray, but had eventually given up and settled into a routine that consisted of flapping, translucent like snippets of fishing line, in the muggy breeze.

On his face sat glasses with thick lenses that had grown foggy over time, like old windows in need of washing.

He was one of those ex-drinkers who stopped because he couldn't be drunk anymore, not out of any particular desire to be sober.

He had been a groundskeeper at the mission for years. During most of that time, he was employed by an old, corpulent monsignor who walked with a cane, wore a long black frock, matching thick-rimmed spectacles, and ruled the grounds in the old-school way of a man who took authority for granted. Joe knew he always had a hammock to sleep in, tucked safely in the back of the utility shed, a little electric stove for cooking, and a hose for bathing. He could live in the shed, reading by the light of a dozen votive candles, whenever he wished. He would disappear for weeks, months, or even years.

Sitting atop a box of rosaries, he told me of the days when he and his friends would get smashed on pilfered sacramental wine and eat hot dogs and beans; a late-night feast cooked over an open fire while the rest of the city slept.

Joe cared for the monsignor's dogs, a pair of slobbering, jovial black labs, and the holy man would always drop off bags of human food alongside the monthly supply of kibble.

When the monsignor died, the operation was taken over by a new kind of man. Trim and neat, with the ever-calculating mind of a businessman. Gone were the days of sacramental wine, hot dogs and drifting the seas as he pleased.

The new boss pointed out, accurately I suppose, that Joe was guilty of the sin of laziness.

I always thought of Joe as charming. A character from Steinbeck's Cannery Row come to life a few decades too late and on the wrong coast. The type of character Hemingway affectionately referred to as a "rummy." The term was descriptive rather than judgmental. The way you'd say someone is "a redhead" or "left-handed."

But Joe's worst trait was that he, among so many other things, was an insurance liability. The boss was convinced his very presence would render management responsible for any accident or injury that occurred on the grounds.

I had once seen him set down, walk away from and eventually abandon entirely a running chainsaw. So maybe the boss had a point.

Still, Joe seemed like part of the mission. Its history was one of Indian chiefs, Spanish conquistadors, English and French invaders, cholera, massacres and weddings, holy men and murderers. It was a place where women from across the world, incapable of conceiving children, would travel to pray in front of the lady of the milk and happy delivery. In a world where Joe clearly didn't quite fit in, the mission, with its mishmash of saints and sinners, seemed like an apt home.

Years later, I called to see if they still sold a short historical booklet I wrote about the mission and shrine. They did, the boss told me.

"And I thought you would want to know," he added. "Joe is gone."

I doubt Joe thrived away from the comforting sulfur smells and mystical sights of his makeshift home. But I hope that when he died, some of his pirate buddies found a way to secretly bury him in that old graveyard – among victims of yellow fever, black plague and arrow wounds. He could lie among all those sinners who arrived on a boat from Spain, many years ago. He seemed like he would fit right in.

They say it's a place where miracles have happened before, that little grove of headstones on the shore of a pristine inlet.

HAVING A COW

When your wife is very pregnant, comparing her to a cow won't make her feel any better. At least, that's what the doctor told me.

In my defense, I grew up on a farm. Most of my prior experiences with pregnancy and delivery took place on carpets of straw, in old barns imbued with the saccharine odor of silage and cobwebs. Little bovine lives seemed to begin only in the dead of night, like some arcane ritual when the world was palpably different and every dark shape was malleable and less resistant to your imagination's whims.

My dad would rouse me from bed, leading me out across the chilly, crunchy gravel yard and down to a stall where a cow would stand, sometimes sit. She would strain her leathery flanks, emitting a low, huffing sound as a gangly, mewing calf emerged from deep within her, plopping into the world.

Those were magical nights, when the looming threat of school and classwork, of bullies and girls, of horrific, reconstituted chicken nuggets all melted away. I felt like I lived on another planet, or perhaps in another time, as I watched the steam rise from a baby cow like the wispy tenacity of life incarnate.

It always made the banalities and worries of everyday life seem remote and undaunting.

While my wife was pregnant over the course of a very long winter, I kept thinking back. As she grew, I comforted myself by thinking of those late nights in the maternity barn. Human birth couldn't be that different, I reasoned. And if those little creatures—dropped onto the ground with a thudding lack of ceremony—could survive, then my baby (and maybe even myself) had to at least stand a chance.

The more I thought about it, the better I felt. I remembered that in the hayloft above me on those nights, a motley herd of barn cats were curled up around their various, soggy, blind litters. Some made their way onto the roof of our house, then scratched and tore at the screen on the second floor window to my bedroom, demanding entry. I would groggily acquiesce, flinging the window open and returning to bed. Sometimes, as thanks for my kindness, I would be greeted in the morning by a brand-new litter of kittens, crawling around in a shoebox or on a blanket at the foot of the bed.

I found these memories comforting, and made a point of saying so on our trips to the doctor's office. But my comments, observations and queries seemed to have the opposite effect on our doctor, making him increasingly uncomfortable.

"Cows get that!" I offered cheerily when he warned that nursing mothers sometimes develop an infection called mastitis. "They get that in their udders."

"Sometimes calves try to come out that way," I chimed in with a knowing smile when the doctor advised us about breach births. "My dad usually reached in and tried to turn them around, or used a chain to pull them out."

When the doctor said the first few days can be stressful, I nodded in agreement. "Yup, that's when the coyotes are most likely to strike."

"Don't worry," I added reassuringly. "Our house is predator-proof."

The doctor continued to monitor my wife's physical condition, and that of our unborn daughter. And I couldn't help but notice that he seemed to be keeping a close eye on my mental health as well.

He eventually suggested that I keep my mouth closed for the remainder of the pregnancy. This seemed harsh, but I persevered by reminding myself that, unlike my wife, I could still drink beer and eat cold cuts and fish. (He also left open a gaping loophole when he failed to add any prohibition on writing.)

When our daughter was finally born, my course of treatment ended. I was once again free to speak my mind. It was ironic, because for the first time in my life I felt utterly inarticulate.

Something about my little girl's breath rendered me speechless. I don't mean to insult my friends, but I generally think of breath as an unpleasant balladeer who goes around composing songs about various unsavory deeds that happened earlier in the day, most of them involving onions or hummus.

So when I held our daughter up to my face and she unleashed a dramatic yawn, I was struck by a smell both foreign and comforting. It came from a mouth that had never smoked a cigarette, never drank a cheap beer, had never sworn or said a harsh word to someone in anger. It's a mouth that had never complained about the horrors of being middle class, never munched on junk food, never been pursed tight in anger or swung ajar in sorrow. It had never lied, never complained about the weather on a perfectly nice day, and never sighed in boredom when there were literally millions of brilliant things to see and do in the world.

My wife and I have a long-running joke about how comically insufferable parents are. Get a beer or a glass of wine in them, and out pops this annoying speech that always starts out with, "Until you have a child...". They are, we've always been fairly certain, suffering from an acute case of Stockholm Syndrome, fumbling around for just the right words to explain why their captors are so great.

But now I kind of understand what they were trying to tell me: Hadley Geiger makes all my prior joys and victories seem petty, mundane and inconsequential. Until she was born, my proudest moments were a really long keg-stand I did in college, the time I spelled the word "necessarily" correctly without the assistance of spellcheck, and the time I finished *The Brothers Karamazov* and had a vague idea who roughly half of the characters were.

But with most of my achievements, there was always a lingering smidgen of doubt. The idea that my actions were, at best, morally ambiguous.

Now I know I've done something good.

And that makes me feel a familiar kind of awe. A sensation I hadn't experienced in a quarter century. One that makes tomorrow's obligations and worries feel distant and unreal. It's the feeling I used to get when I stood on a bed of hay in a little stall, late at night, and waited for something amazing to happen.

FLIGHT RISK

My wife and I were recently on an airplane that experienced hydraulic failure 30,000 feet above the icy North Atlantic Ocean. It wasn't even the most terrifying ride I took that day.

It all started when, more than three hours into our flight from Chicago to Ireland, where we planned to begin our vacation, the pilot got on the intercom.

"Uuuggh, I hope you're all settling in nicely," he said. "It appears some of our hydraulics aren't working and this aircraft isn't fit to take across the Atlantic. We're going to have to turn around and take you back to Chicago."

Then, to our dismay, the little digital picture of an airplane that had been tracking our progress on all the cabin's tiny screens pulled an actual, slightly illegal looking U-turn.

"Oh, by the way," the captain added. "This plane has, like, a million backup systems, so there's nothing to worry about."

A lack of attention to detail is okay in many professions. In an abstract painter, for instance, or someone who writes humorous stories for a living.

I find it troubling in an airline pilot. I kept waiting for him to get back on the speaker and add: "Seriously. Don't worry. We're, like, a million miles above the ground."

I also didn't understand why plummeting many miles into the ocean would be any worse than falling to our deaths in, say, Buffalo, New York, on our way back to Chicago. While the former would certainly be cold, wet, and scary, the latter would combine the unfathomable horror of nonexistence with a trip to Buffalo, which is only marginally better.

For the next three hours, something beneath us—something cold, metal and broken—made a perpetual screeching sound.

As we approached O'Hare International Airport, our trusty captain's voice returned. "Okay, everyone. They've set aside the longest runway for us," he said, his voice crackling like that of a radio personality from the 1920s. "It's a thousand miles long."

I looked out the window and saw a tarmac teaming with flashing lights. Police were there to keep the peace while medics hauled away our corpses and firefighters put out the fiery wreckage of the plane, I figured.

Death will come whenever it chooses and you generally don't have much say in the matter. But to spend my final six hours of life sitting in a chair designed for a person 80 pounds lighter than me, digesting a terrible meal produced in a kitchen run by sadists, would be a terrible end to what had been a pretty good life.

I won't even talk about the in-flight movie, except to say that Billy Crystal's Botox-infused face is not the last thing I want to see before I leave this earth.

As you probably guessed due to the fact that I was able to write this story, we landed uneventfully to the sound of hearty clapping. We were then towed to the gate, which was not even close to being a thousand miles away.

Inside the airport at 4 a.m., we learned we would have to book a new flight and try again in several hours.

The thing that kept me going—the thing to which I clung with mad desire—was my indignation. Until it was stolen by a large Indian family sitting on the floor to my right. And by a young American woman to my left.

You see, I was traveling to Ireland to drink slightly blacker beer while gazing at slightly greener fields.

"I was supposed to be in a pub in Dublin by now!" I grumbled to my wife. "This is the worst day of my life."

The family to my right glanced up, the father replying: "We are supposed to be attending my sister's wedding, but it appears we won't make the connecting flight." In his arms he cradled a tiny baby who was bawling in the same manner I was.

"I'm going to miss my connection, too," said the young women to my left. "And I'm supposed to be building an orphanage in Ghana tomorrow."

"Great," I thought. *"Now I can't even complain without sounding petulant."* After all, my problems were decidedly of the First World variety—essentially issues of discomfort.

My wife and I headed to a hotel on the other side of the city. There, we relaxed by glaring at (but definitely not touching) some kind of ash tray/bed amalgamation in our room. Then we ate an alleged continental breakfast, which had been flown in from the little-known continent of Starchica, which is populated entirely by melancholy, slightly lethargic people.

Then we decided to head back to the airport to try our luck again.

As I sat down in the back of our cab, I had no idea I was about to embark on the most terrifying ride of my life.

Our driver fumbled with a large, yellowed Tupperware container as she drove. Then her cell phone rang. It's hard to interpret one side of a conversation when you can't hear the interlocutor, so I'll just share what I heard on my end:

"Yup… Cans… My gallbladder is acting up again… That was my husband."

When she hung up, our driver redoubled her efforts to open the mysterious, jaundiced plastic container. After she ran a second red light, I reached forward and offered to open it for her.

With my gallbladder functioning at 100 percent and no steering wheel to distract me, I was able to open the container in a few seconds. In retrospect it was a mistake.

Inside the box sat a row of white hot dog buns, all of which contained what I really hope was baloney. These grayish, vaguely pink slices were doused in mayonnaise and had clearly been left to fester in the hot vehicle for quite some time.

I masked a gagging sound by pretending to cough, quickly handing the sandwiches to our driver.

As she ate, I tried to converse with her.

"So, you must meet a lot of interesting people while driving a cab in this city," I said. "Right?"

"Not really," she grunted. "I met one. He was a golfer. I didn't like him."

Stuck at a conversational impasse, I glanced out the window and stared at all the cars we were about to hit.

Our driver was unable to remember the exact result produced by pressing each of the car's two pedals. The result was that every time we needed to accelerate or come to a stop, there was a 50 percent chance she would slam down on the wrong one with her foot. After a moment in which we were either hurtling toward stopped traffic or grinding to a halt in the fast lane, she would realize the problem and switch pedals.

The steering wheel was similarly enigmatic for our driver. She seemed to believe it worked on some kind of mysterious, inverted axis. The result was that every left turn was a little panicky, preceded as it was by a very hard jerk to the right.

Her sandwiches consumed, she settled in and focused all of her energy on driving with the kind of energy a fly has when it comes up against a glass window.

I figured another polite attempt at conversation was worth a shot.

"Do you have any idea how much further it is?" I queried.

"Yeah," she said through a ferocious burp. "It's seven more miles, exactly."

I glanced over at my wife, who had terror in her eyes. I smiled and mouthed the words: "We're going to be fine."

MY BABY EATS DOG FOOD

My wife and I like to eat organic meats and vegetables. Our 10-month-old daughter prefers dog food.

Our dining preferences stem from a desire to do what's best for our bodies and the land. Plus—let's be honest here—we have a strong desire to look down our noses at people who think $19 is an outrageous price to pay for a single turnip.

"Look at those nice brown spots," I say, tossing a head of lettuce into our shopping cart. "And all the holes where bugs grazed on it. This has definitely never seen a pesticide."

Hadley's hunger for kibble is a mystery to us. She prefers them round, windpipe-sized and preferably slathered in an assortment of household detritus. When she's feeling particularly fancy, she likes to dip them into the slimy depths of the dog's water dish—au jus, we call this—before popping them into her mouth.

We regularly spend 15 to 20 minutes scouring the Internet to find out if any baby anywhere has ever been allergic to each specific food before introducing it to her diet. (I can save you the trouble: the answer is "yes.")

But we always have to scurry away from the computer when we suddenly realize our daughter—born so pure, such a short time ago—is in the other room, gnawing on a pellet of corn gluten meal and chicken by-products. On the plus side, she's getting a whopping dose of glucosamine in case she develops hip dysplasia when she reaches the ripe old age of 10 or 11.

People without kids sometimes tell me their dogs are like their children. To them, I will now respond: "Well, my child is a lot like my dog."

The first time she did it, I leaned down and read the back of the bag. "Says here it's for all life stages," I said to myself. "And it provides 'complete and balanced nutrition.' That's good."

I sped up, choosing not to dwell on the part where it pledged to contain enough omega fatty acids to produce a nice, shiny coat.

I've had friends judge me for feeding regular dog food to my dog. "Have you any idea what's in that stuff?" they say with a roll of the eyes. "I make my dog's food from scratch because I have literally unlimited money, and I exist outside of the space/time continuum so I have endless hours to devote to ridiculous endeavors." I'm not 100 percent certain that's what they said, but that is what I heard.

I hope these same friends don't find out my daughter is munching on food out of a 50-pound bag.

But, as the old saying goes, a baby cannot live by dog food alone.

While my wife and I engage in long, drawn out, Israel/Palestine-esque debates about whether it's okay to feed our baby things like organic strawberries, we look around and realize she is quietly and contentedly sitting in the corner, watching us with befuddled amusement and munching on a handful of fern leaves.

Her motives, as with all things, remain a mystery. I'm assuming once she starts talking, she will illuminate a collection of behaviors that currently adhere to no discernible rhyme or reason.

"I like things that are 'chicken flavored,' and the only food you leave on the ground in a bag where I can reach it, is for canines," she'll explain. "I work with what you give me."

"I pooped on the wall and screamed at you night after night because I'm a sadist, Dad," are also some of the first words I expect her to utter.

Unfortunately, I have no idea when she'll master language, because every parent I talk to is holding their cards pretty close to the chest on the matter.

"It varies so much," they all say, avoiding specifics like an Iowa-bound political candidate. "She could start saying words tomorrow, or a year from now."

In the meantime, I'm using every ounce of self-control to avoid babbling incoherently to my baby. "Baby talk," according to most intelligent people I know, is a bad thing. "She should be copying you," they explain. "You shouldn't be copying her."

It's sound advice, but I'm finding myself ill-suited to the task of teaching English to a diminutive lunatic who would rather climb a bookshelf than take notes on grammar.

Proper instruction is the type of thing I used to hear in the grocery store—the type of thing that made me swear not to have children. People so intent on describing the world around them in easily understandable terms that they say things like: "This is a box of cereal, Johnny. It's yellow, and rectangular, and made of cardboard. I'm putting it in the shopping cart. The shopping cart is made of metal, and it has wheels."

People speak to their small children as if they are narrating an incredibly boring movie for the sight-impaired. "These are socks. Now I'm putting them on my feet," they blather. "Now I'm getting the mail out of the mailbox. Now I'm throwing the newspaper in the recycling bin."

"Now I'm falling down the stairs because you left your toy tractor on the top step…"

Parenthood can turn someone born and raised in Cleveland into the verbal equivalent of a tourist anxious to test out a few weeks of English lessons in the real world.

"That's a car!" they shout, gesturing toward a Subaru. "And over there is a cat! Pleased to meet you, cat, thank you and goodbye!"

The most difficult part for me is that the English language is staggeringly inconsistent. There are so many different sets of rules, and just as many exceptions to those. The more cognizant you are of these rules, the more difficult it is to speak English without fretting constantly about your grammar.

Should I teach her to speak in the Chicago/Turabian style, putting footnotes at the end of my sentences? Would Modern Language Association rules best prepare her for postmodern life? Should I say "towards," with an "s," according to the Oxford English rules, or "toward," without the "s," in accordance with Associated Press guidelines?

I sound like an idiot when I speak to her. "This is a chair," I explain. "This is for sitting on... er, something on which you sit... uh, something in which you sit... actually, please get off the chair—out of the chair, I mean—and put down the book of matches and spit out the dog food."

The only thing I'm teaching her at this point is that her father's grasp on his native language is tenuous, and his mind often wanders.

I'd honestly love to engage in a little baby talk from time to time, if only to rest my weary mind. Maybe this relationship can be about give and take—about two people of very different weights learning mutually from one another. Maybe we can sit, side by side—her with a little plate of dog food and fern leaves, me with my turnip—and we can share stories with each other.

Most adult conversations are filled with nonsense, anyway. At least with my daughter, I'll be thoroughly enjoying myself, babbling away with someone whose stories don't even need to contain real words in order to captivate me.

A HORSE WITH A MOHAWK

O ne day, my parents woke up to the bleak realization they were middle-aged.

To make matters worse, their only son, a boy they so hoped would set the academic world on fire, was showing signs he was far more apt to set blazes of the literal, accidental variety.

A midlife crisis is many things, but at its core it's just the realization that you could die tomorrow and there's a chance people would simply chalk it up to "natural causes."

Some parents react with dignified resignation. In these cases, one of them, usually the father, moves into an underutilized room, often a basement or attic. Then the two adults begin fervently pursuing strange hobbies, because they no longer care what people think of them now that they've pondered their own mortality.

Dad suddenly takes up the drums, much to the dismay of everyone in the neighborhood with aural faculties. Mom finally sits down to write an unabashedly self-indulgent first novel about a strong, independent woman whose family doesn't appreciate her.

Others, staring into the abyss and realizing their spouse will someday die—perhaps before the next president is elected—begin a preemptive strike, getting divorced so the only death they'll ever have to cope with is their own.

Still others plan a long vacation together. This is done with the vague hope that a slightly different climate or local cuisine will somehow make undesirable personality traits more bearable. *"Perhaps I won't care about his foot odor if the weather is warmer,"* the wife thinks to herself as they buy plane tickets.

Others, and God bless my parents for falling into this nifty category, simply do the craziest thing they can think of. They tend to do this as a committed, slightly wild-eyed team.

After all, young people's best-known quality is their uncanny knack for making bad decisions. What better way to remain youthful than to display terrible decision-making skills for the whole world to see?

This is why I woke up one morning and discovered two horses, each sporting a tall black and white Mohawk, standing in a paddock outside my childhood home.

After a brief discussion, I slowly (and a little nervously) came to understand that my mom and dad had decided to start collecting a rare breed of prehistoric-looking horse that hails for Scandinavia.

It all started with my father's preoccupation with our heritage. My grandfather's family was of Swiss origin, but we were already paying tribute to that lineage by acting kind of snooty.

My grandmother was Norwegian. It was in an attempt to get in touch with those roots that my parents started bringing home Norwegian Fjord horses. The stocky, thick-coated animals are dun in color. They have existed as a domesticated breed for approximately 4000 years. According to the Norwegian Fjord Horse Registry, they've roamed wild in Norway since the last Ice Age, and their remains have been discovered at excavations of Viking sites.

A typical Fjord has a mane that is black in the middle and white on the sides. The coarse hair is traditionally cut short.

This serves two purposes. The first is to prompt the hair to stand upright in a crescent shape that accentuates the curve of the horse's neck beneath it. The second is to accentuate the questionable mental acuity of the horse's owners.

Basically the mane is the equine equivalent of one of those "I'm With Stupid" t-shirts. The finger was pointing squarely at my parents.

They even got a young horse for me. It was a female named Hester, whose coat was more ruddy than that of most of her companions.

When they announced over breakfast their plans to start collecting these horses, my parents had spoken at great length about the breed's legendary toughness. According to my mother, they never got sick, could carry preposterous amounts of weight, and loved to work in the same docile way human beings love watching TV.

Imagine my surprise when Hester, at the age of two, keeled over one morning, falling stone dead against a fence. The killer was an aneurism.

This episode taught me many things, but two stuck with me. The first was that everything dies, usually sooner than you expect. The second was that my parents often had no idea what they were talking about.

I was in sixth grade when Hester died, and I stayed home from school that day. My dad used a tractor to dig a hole, placing her carcass inside as gently as the heavy machinery would allow. He covered it with a blanket of fresh soil and a massive rock.

"This way nothing will dig her up and eat her," observed my father, hands on his hips, ever the farmer, ever the realist.

Seeing her dead was bad enough, he reasoned. I didn't need to wake up the next morning to discover a pack of coyotes feasting on her entrails in the field behind our house.

My biggest problem with my parents' decision to get into the Fjord Horse subculture was not that it drained my college fund, nor that it promised no foreseeable payoff other than the accomplished feeling one gets from paying large vet bills.

The problem, in my eyes, was that my parents had chosen to own such a weird breed of horse.

"Why can't you guys just get normal horses?" I complained. "Even a standard horse would probably get me teased at school, but you had to go get these things that look like they arrived directly from the Pleistocene Epoch."

It was always a source of shame for me that our horses weren't normal. The fact that their hair didn't look like the hair of all the horses I saw in movies drove me to despair.

"Can I see the horses?" my suburban friends would ask.

"There's nothing to see in there," I'd lament, eyeing the barn sadly. "Those horses are nerds, just like my mom and dad."

My parents surely felt the exact same way about me. They often sent me away on unnecessary, but extremely time-consuming errands whenever they had visitors. My hair, which was died pink at the time, along with my multiple body piercings probably had something to do with it.

I'm sure my parents, when watching television, wondered: "Why doesn't our kid look like the kids in this sitcom? Why, oh why, can't he be normal?"

For my part, I was terrified the Fjords were simply the beginning. The first little pebble beginning its descent down the precipice of a very slippery, very dorky slope.

Whenever I checked on the cows, I'd breathe a sigh of relief when none of them suddenly had gaudy tattoos or leather jackets. It wouldn't have surprised me if they had.

I'd forgotten all about the Fjords until I went to fall festival in a small town many years later. I spotted a round pen containing two horses that looked as if they were from the Ice Age. On top of their necks were rigid, carefully crafted Mohawks. The black center stripe was trimmed a little longer than the white sides.

A little girl was reaching eagerly through the bars to feed them some hay. "These horses are really cool," she informed her parents in a matter-of-fact tone. "Way cooler than those boring ones you normally see on TV."

"Yeah," I suddenly realized. "I guess they are."

BEFORE I GO

I used to have a Darwinian view on parenting. Like all uninformed opinions, it was elegant in its simplicity.

"Kids have survived for thousands of generations without car seats, helmets, vaccines or organic, lavender-scented diaper cream," I said. "I'm pretty sure the survival of our species proves we don't need to go out of our way to keep them alive."

What I immediately realized the first time I looked at my daughter was the fundamental difference between the species as a whole—which includes billions of people, many of whom are murdering, stealing and singing karaoke at this very moment—and my little girl, who is currently gnawing on my leg and saying "meow" while pointing at a picture of a pig.

It's not that I don't care about the whole of humanity. It's that I care about it far less than I care about the little girl whose health, safety and ultimate happiness are my responsibility.

People often think they can save the world. They tend to wave a lot of signs and litter your Facebook wall with their political sentiments, but they are really just wasting time. Shout at your political foes all you want about who you plan to vote for. It won't do anything to make the world better or worse; it will just make it more annoying.

But I can, in theory at least, save one small, wide-eyed person who is drinking in everything I say and do.

If everyone did, humanity would need a lot less fixing. The good of the few, I'm starting to think, actually does outweigh the good of the many.

On the Origin of Species, my former parenting guide, is looking increasingly like a scientific text with surprisingly little to say on whether my daughter, Hadley, should be allowed to eat a mummified granola bar of indeterminate origin that she found on the sidewalk.

Plus, billions and billions of children actually HAVE died during our species' time on earth. Botulism, small pox, kitchen accidents, microscopic organisms, other children, cold, heat, elephants—even paper cuts—have claimed the lives of countless individual kids.

While the species has survived—flourished, even—that success has been on a macro-scale. Enough DNA has been passed forward to keep us alive as a species.

The fate of individuals has been far more varied.

So my current goal is far more personal, more modest, yet more daunting than saving the world: I want one brown-eyed girl, with wild locks that look like they were styled by the antediluvian winds of the Mongolian steppes, to grow safely into adulthood. I'll leave the fate of humanity up to priests, politicians and people who have nothing better to do with their time.

A dark shadow tags along behind this mission. A second thought that is inexorably linked to the first: I will die.

It's a fact that used to seem like a minor inconvenience. But since I've always viewed myself as a net burden on society—specifically on my loved ones—my eventual demise seemed like it would be a bit of a mixed bag. Society, I was modest enough to realize, could probably withstand the loss of a single, tubby white male. There are others, after all.

"If I make it to 40, I'll feel I've had a good run," I used to tell my friends. "I'll consider anything after that to be bonus, encore years on earth."

But that was all before I had such an important job to do.

And as I write this, the thought of perishing gives me a cold, hollow feeling deep within my gut. It's a fear that makes my limbs feel weak and my vision blurry. It bludgeons me when I hear certain trigger words—"cancer," "heart disease," "car crash," "spontaneous combustion"— and it is a very new sensation.

My life is no longer a jaunty experiment in Taoist living. It is now the means to an end. I need to deftly guide Hadley into adulthood, and I don't have my old, Darwinian philosophy to quell all my fears.

Sure, humanity will survive for thousands more years. But more importantly, how many more years will I be here to grab her as she's about to fall down the stairs.

My daughter is not the sound of a tree falling in the woods. She will go on after me. She will exist, assuming no greater tragedy, when I no longer do. She is of me, but independent of me. But her chances are better with me standing guard, a vaguely ursine sentinel who more often than not is eating some kind of cheese while keeping a watchful eye on his daughter.

But someday I will cease to exist here on the temporal plane, and I will begin a new life within the mind of my daughter. The Matt Geiger who survives in the minds of others who have known me will be a pleasant apparition, I hope, but nothing more than deformed shadows on the wall of a cave. They will be mere echoes of the real me. The real me will reside for the rest of her life in Hadley Geiger's thoughts, hopes, fears and aspirations.

I've never known a feeling as real, as visceral, as the warm strength that fills my musculature when my daughter, spooked by the barking of a dog or afraid of a bug's sting, runs to me for comfort. It is the only sensation I've ever experienced that is more powerful that the cold, empty weakness that creeps in when I ponder my death.

When it first occurred to me that someday I might not be there when she turns and looks for somewhere to run, I decided to get life insurance.

The process was filled with unpleasantness. Partially because it involves mortality. But also because it required paperwork, which I dread even more than death.

The process also included a physical, during which my inevitable death was the primary focus.

"Good morning!" said the nurse administering the exam. "How are you today?"

Her chipper tone was bizarre considering the reason for her visit. This was a woman who was looking at me, drawing my blood and asking me various questions in order to try to approximate how much longer I get to live. She was being paid, like some macabre carnival attraction, to guess the day on which I would draw my final breath.

Even when I passed the physical and received my insurance policy, my relief was fleeting.

"Oh, good, I'm healthy," I thought. "For now..."

I was so bothered by the idea that I will someday leave Hadley for good, that I headed into my library and decided to create a special shelf just for my daughter. On it, I lined up 15 books. Roughly 8,000 pages of wisdom that helped make me who I am today.

On a small piece of scrap paper, I wrote *Books for Hadley to read*, taping the label to the shelf in the hopes that one day—hopefully a very distant one—she can begin to make her way through the ideas I cherish. That way, when the physical me is gone, the Matt who lives on as an idea in my daughter's mind will have company.

Gabriel Garcia Márquez, Cormac McCarthy, Fyodor Dostoyevsky, Ernest Hemingway, Karl Ove Knausgaard and Lao Tsu will all be there to fill her head with beautiful, complicated, contradictory ideas.

They are and will remain real, existing beyond their physical forms. And if they can achieve such immortality, maybe I can, too. We, with our cool beards and weird thoughts, can be roommates in my daughter's brain— always there for her to turn to when she gets scared or curious.

The great thing about being a hypochondriac is that eventually you are proven right. Sure, you die like everyone else, but you get to die vindicated, which is the best way to go. Being right, after all, is an infrequent phenomenon and should therefore be savored.

"I knew that cough sounded ominous," I'll think as life someday slips from my grasp, adding a sentence I rarely had the pleasure to utter during my more vibrant years: "I was right!"

In the meantime, I keep experiencing waves of optimism that have no concrete explanation. With every day Hadley is still here to bite me, eat stale granola bars, and make adorable but wildly inaccurate taxonomical classifications, I feel more at ease with life, and even with death.

She listens to everything I say, so I tell her that she should glow with optimism, because never again will she have so much life stretched out in front of her. So much vast possibility. So many opportunities to feel joy, sorrow, and even those boring feelings in between.

In fact, her mere presence has taught me an important lesson.

Because with every moment we spend together, she makes me understand that I will never again have so much life stretched out before me. However much time I have in front of me right this second, it is more than I will ever have again.

I don't know exactly how much it is—it could be 50 years, or it could be five minutes. But it will remain true until I draw my final breath.

THANK YOU, ALABAMA

I spent a series of Thanksgivings in Alabama, with the family of my college girlfriend. The primary advantage of doing this was that I could avoid choosing which of my recently divorced parents to visit.

Sara, my girlfriend, had a father with a bald head orbited by an unruly fringe of gray hair. His ears were pronounced and stuck out like the ones that come with a Mr. Potato Head toy. I liked to think they had experienced a late-in-life growth spurt in a desperate attempt to keep up with the size of the hearing aids he wore, which were each the shape, color and size of a giraffe's kidney, and seemed to have increased in girth every time I saw him.

He was an engineer by trade, working tirelessly to develop absorbents that could soak up oil that had been carelessly spilled into the ocean. He had been forced into retirement from his prior job due to budget cuts, and had taken a new position in Mississippi.

He had little choice. One child was an undergraduate, which was costly. The other was entering law school, which was even costlier. Plus, the family gave much of what they earned each year to charity, which must have seriously cut into their savings.

So each Monday at 4 a.m., he would climb into his diminutive pickup truck and drive more than 3 hours to his office, staying at a shoddy hotel all week and returning late Friday night.

A smile was his default facial expression, perhaps so he wouldn't appear dim or ill-humored if someone told a joke his hearing aids did not pick up. He also liked to tell people his profession along with his name, which made him sound as if he were perpetually introducing himself at an Alcoholics Anonymous meeting.

"Hi, my name is Mark and I'm an engineer," he would say in an amplified baritone prone to cracking.

"Hi Mark; I'm Trey and I'm a waiter," our server at a local seafood restaurant once replied.

It was as if engineers were a distinct subspecies of human and everyone was entitled to fair warning that the standard rules of etiquette would not apply to the ensuing interaction.

In any event, it helped explain Mark's habit of being fascinated by anything that had moving parts. He would frequently stop and linger to ponder the latch on a neighbor's gate, which certainly made more than a few people make a mental note to lock the doors that night.

Sometimes he would pick up and examine a toy truck being played with by a child in the town park.

"Well, will you look at that," he would announce, poking at some small moving part with his finger. "Ingenious!"

Sara's mother, Abby, was a nurse who ranked college football only slightly below God on her list of priorities. She habitually collected pecans from a cluster of trees in their yard, and would shell them by hand whenever watching television, reading a book or holding a conversation around the house. She frequently paused to pop one into her mouth, and the habit, along with her short gray hair, made her look vaguely like a 120-pound squirrel that had gotten in through the attic and decided to pursue winter preparations in the kitchen.

Mark was what we in the college's philosophy and religion department called a literalist, meaning he interpreted the Bible as a literal document rather than a set of allegorical stories. As a result, he was perpetually and eagerly awaiting the Messiah's impending return.

This meant no matter who rang the doorbell, Mark was always a little underwhelmed when he answered it to find a mortal standing on the other side.

"Je... Oh, hey Matt," he'd say as he swung the door open. He was polite, but you just knew the unemployed C-student dating his daughter was a disappointing house-guest—especially when he had clearly been expecting God incarnate.

I wanted to apologize, but there was little I could say. I couldn't heal the sick or walk on water. All I ever managed to do at their home was to pile up dirty laundry and forget to shut the gate, thereby allowing the family dog to escape.

Each Sunday morning, we all traveled to a pastel pink, non-denominational mini-church. Members of the congregation were the parents of most of the people who hung out at the local senior center.

The church was situated in an expansive countryside, surrounded by grazing humpbacked cattle that would lazily swish their tales through the autumn air.

Inside the church, Mark could worship in peace, knowing he was not wearing the only (or even the largest) hearing aids in the room.

The pastor of the church, Dan, had landed the job when his predecessor, who had apparently time traveled there from the 1890s, managed to weave the term "colored" into one too many sermons. Dan was a retired military man who had kept his youthful crew cut and his sinewy 18-year-old legs. In between, he was cultivating a vast midsection.

Presumably angered by increasingly strenuous working conditions, the pastor's heart decided one day to suddenly go on strike. This caused the pastor to cease living for a few seconds, but he was quickly resuscitated and soon underwent bypass surgery.

Sara's parents responded to human need like dogs to a whistle, and they invited the pastor and his wife to join us for Thanksgiving dinner. This was a tad ironic, we soon learned, because following his surgery, the good reverend's body dropped instantly into a deep slumber whenever his metabolism was called upon to digest food.

In essence, Thanksgiving dinner was a reenactment of the movie *Weekend at Bernie's*, with a limp body being moved from room to room with us throughout the day, always propped up on a chair or leaning against a cupboard.

In the kitchen, Dan sampled from a bowl of mixed nuts, then swiftly dozed off, resting his face on a small, checkered, blue-and-white tabletop in the corner of the room.

At dinner, someone passed the gravy boat too close to the underside of his nose and he instantly reclined in his chair, his head lolling back, intermittent snores and grunts emanating from his lips.

After the meal, he abandoned pretense and took a nap in a recliner by the fireplace, with an afghan draped over his lap. His wife would frequently reach over and check his pulse, then cover his arm back up with the blanket.

Sara's mother was one of the best cooks I've ever known. She made everything from scratch, using mostly southern recipes, and she made it in copious quantities.

Even on a regular Saturday, you could hear her mixing the dry ingredients with the butter in the morning and anticipate the fresh cookies, which she insisted everyone sample later that day. She managed to prepare a wide array of courses almost exclusively in heavy glass casserole dishes, and she had no desire to make her food appear healthy or refined.

When sweet potatoes were served, they were tucked in beneath a thick blanket of bubbling marshmallows, with butter seeping out through every crack. At her table, when your right paw handed off a plate of meat or biscuits, your left was simultaneously receiving the gravy.

Simply bursting with charity and good will, Sara's parents had a tradition of pushing plate after plate of food before guests to make sure everyone got their fill. It was almost as if they always cooked enough food for one additional guest who hadn't eaten in 2000 years.

I, on the other hand, was raised not to leave food on my plate, especially when I was an unpaying houseguest and the dog was still missing.

Needless to say, these two family traditions did not mix well: I didn't want to stop eating until my plate was clean, and they worked zealously to keep food in front of me. The cycle would have been comical were it not for the barely living human reminder of the dangers of heart disease who was snoring away in the seat next to me.

The year the pastor ate with us, things got out of hand and toward the end of the meal, I looked up and realized a room full of people had been watching, with a combination of horror and awe, as I ate several pounds of food. A celebration of the harvest had turned into a well-intentioned, but painful, display of gluttony, the likes of which tradition-ally take place beneath a tent, with a roped-off entrance at which someone in a top hat rips ticket stubs.

When it was finally over, we all walked—I waddled, to be more accurate—into the living room, where I curled up in the chair next to the pastor and went to sleep.

With every ounce of blood in my body coursing toward my gut, none was left to power my brain, so I didn't even remember to call either of my parents, which happily helped me stay completely fair in my treatment of both of them on that wonderful holiday.

NAKED BRUNCH

There was a kid in the neighborhood where I grew up who kept losing his clothes.

Birthday parties, family dinners, church picnics, school recess: it mattered not. Regardless of the setting, the weather, or the company, he would inevitably streak through it.

At first, it seemed reasonable. We were very young and clothing was often perplexing. We were physically incapable of putting on several pieces of our daily ensembles. Shoes were a mystery, hats were a bit over our heads, and pants were an enigma with razor-sharp zippers that nipped at our weak flesh.

At that early age, it seemed understandable that our friend sometimes wriggled out of this attire. Perhaps, we wondered as he took a seat on the swing set and swung back and forth with an added level of drama, his parents had let him dress himself and he experienced a catastrophic wardrobe malfunction that left him naked and, as far as we could tell, completely unaware of the fact.

As we aged, gaining the physical and mental dexterity to dress ourselves, our friend continued losing his clothes. Gatherings always disintegrated into a group Search and Rescue operation where children and parents fanned out, beating the bushes with sticks, urging pet dogs to sniff out absent garments.

Our good-natured friend took part in these searches, and he seemed as befuddled as the rest of us when it came to the location of his pants. When confronted, he adopted a facial expression that suggested intense thought, like someone who has been asked to explain the meaning of life or recite pi to the 100th decimal point. He eventually confirmed that yes, he had, at one point, been wearing far more items than he was now. Then he would run away.

In the eyes of many parents, he had to be stopped. But their passive-aggressive comments bounced off his bare flesh. Some mothers went a step further, wrapping him in a blanket, like some victim being hauled away by the Red Cross at the site of an embassy bombing or a tornado.

Perhaps what puzzled them most was that, unlike victims of terrorism and natural disaster, he was perfectly happy.

And he was an odd-looking fellow. Rotund and freckled, with a porcine snout and an audacious, dirty blond mullet that he could, regrettably, never shed with the rest of his attire.

It was at a sleepover at his house that I discovered the problem was hereditary. Their home was like a little nudist colony, where people ambled about, unhindered by itchy cotton fabric, munching on pretzels and sipping little cups of apple juice. Incidentally, there were gargantuan grains of salt nestled into every single crevice in that home, which seemed unfortunate given all the nudity.

They were harmless, but their home was monumentally different from the one where I spent most of my time. A place populated by good, decent people who were ashamed of their bodies and wore shirts, pants, and sometimes even hats and shoes.

As it turns out, many of the people around me had strange habits and customs. It wasn't limited to nudity.

Some of my other friends looked nothing like one of their parents, which always prompted me to blurt: "Wow, you look absolutely nothing like your dad."

To their credit, I don't recall them taking offense to the observation. They would simply respond with a nonchalant, "That's because my real dad lives in Arizona and now my mom is married to this other guy named Kevin."

Other friends had entire families who were from some far-off land I hadn't yet learned about in school, which always led me to nervously inquire whether they knew what they were doing while they were cooking dinner. Again, they were always graceful, saying things like, "I'm pretty sure I do. Have you not smelled curry before, Matt?"

Yet another friend had asthma, and I don't mean the kind that makes people wheeze a little. This kid had an exciting variety, requiring him to stay near an enormous futuristic contraption at all times, just in case his lungs completely seized up. His house, simply because of the possibility this machine might be rolled out at any time, was a favorite destination for many children. Despite his affliction, he was somehow far better than me at baseball, which stung my ego a bit.

So I spent much of my youth wandering around, noticing things about other families that seemed different or odd, then offering advice about how they could change, become more like me, and nestle in beneath the warm blanket of normality.

Yet I'm sure my house was just as strange in everyone else's eyes. I had the distinction of living on a farm in an area where there was little agricultural land, so my house was different in the way it looked and smelled, and many of my friends appeared both shocked and horrified to find out animals didn't wear pants.

In that way, I suppose they were a lot like one of my human friends.

THE HOUSEGUEST

One afternoon when I was five years old, my mother approached me. She knelt down and peered at me eye to eye, her gaze silent and serious.

I was busy conducting a series of controlled experiments to determine which household objects were willing to ignite when placed atop our ancient bathroom radiator. I thought I recognized the expression on my mom's face.

"Which one of our pets died?" I asked, removing a small, decorative pillow from the radiator and disappointedly placing a mark next to the "did not burn" column on my mental checklist.

"No, Matthew," she said, touching my arm tenderly. "All the pets are fine."

This was a lie. A small Pekinese dog my parents had brought home from the pound a few months earlier had recently been discovered in the form of a flattened, irregular disk in the middle of our gravel driveway. Tufts of red hair on the mammoth tire of a nearby tractor told part of the tale.

But Rosy had been deceased for several weeks, and in the bathroom, next to the radiator, my mother had entirely different news. My parents, perhaps after assessing the unfortunate amalgamation of genes that produced me, were getting another child.

"Your father and I have decided to adopt a baby," my mom said. "You're going to have a little sister. She's flying all the way from Korea."

I tried with my limited verbal repertoire to explain that she was not describing a sister. This sounded more like a person of no relation who would be living under the same roof as us, eating our food and possibly playing with my toys.

The proper nomenclature for someone who does these things is "roommate," "freeloader" or "usurper." "Not 'sister,' " I explained.

This person wouldn't even be able to act as a housing unit for replacement body parts in case I was involved in an accident and needed a new kidney or lung, which I always thought was one of the perks of having a sibling who shared your genetic makeup.

I was, nonetheless, exhilarated to learn that human beings could be ordered from overseas and delivered to our home. I planned to ask for the agency's phone number so that I could order eight more kids and field a full baseball team, but my parents told me it was a lengthy and exhaustive process.

"We had to do a lot of interviews and fill out a ton of paperwork," my dad commented with just a touch of fatigue. "The agency needs to make sure we're good parents. They check references and speak at length with your friends and family."

I found this odd, since no one had bothered to check with me. I could have enumerated several flaws in my parents' work. I would have started by detailing the unfortunate ends met by some of our pets.

I later learned that Ron and Suzy, two close friends of my parents whom we sometimes visited in their noisy Washington, DC apartment, had failed to obtain an adopted baby. The difficulty arose when Ron made the mistake of placing the words "a few bottles of wine" after the question, "How many alcoholic beverages do you typically consume in a day?" on one of the forms.

"I guess they would rather give a baby to a liar than someone who appreciates good wine," Ron later lamented to my father.

My parents went to great lengths to prepare for my sister's arrival. First they read up on Korean culture. Then they purchased books, artwork and clothing meant to make the infant feel at home. The result was that our house looked like a vaguely Asian-themed restaurant.

They named her Cassandra, demoting her native "birth name" down one notch, relegating it to middle name status. My mother tried to rationalize the change.

"This new name will make her feel like part of our family," she said.

My dad was, as usual, more blunt: "Her name happens to sound exactly like the words 'me ran,' and we don't want to give kids in school any excuses to make fun of her heritage. Kids can be cruel and we figured it would be better if her name didn't contain any noun/verb combinations."

Somewhat surprisingly, I knew nothing about Korea, north or south.

Throughout my childhood, my parents had filled our house with exchange students from abroad. It was as if a little United Nations summit for teenagers was taking place in our living room, but the Korean delegates had been unable to attend.

People from Japan, China, Switzerland, Scotland and Germany had all lived with us. The goal had been to expose me to different cultures and discourage the growth of xenophobic or racist sentiments in my burgeoning personality.

But the result was that my young mind judged the populations of entire countries based on the behavior of miserable, pimple-ridden teenage individuals who slept in the room down the hall. For starters, everyone from other countries seemed to be going through an awkward phase.

All Swiss people were bossy and dyed their hair blond, I surmised. Everyone from Japan liked to get drunk and mangle my dad's bicycle by riding it directly into a fence in the middle of the night. Scottish women didn't shave their armpits, smelled of patchouli oil, wore sundresses and jewelry that produced clacking noises. They also gave by far the best piggyback rides.

Chinese people became close friends with my father and spent all of their time talking about agribusiness with him rather than playing with me, causing them to receive low marks in accordance with my grading system.

But I hadn't met anyone from Korea yet, so I wasn't ready to sum up that entire culture in a glib sentence or two.

The irony, of course, is that while she was born in Korea, my little sister is the most prototypical American I have ever met. Today, when I visit her Facebook page, I see references to a mob of celebrities and reality television personalities about whom I have no knowledge.

She frequently abbreviates the names for things, saying them in a pronounced New England accent.

"Let's go grab some burgers at Mickey Dee's," she'll say as we drive by a McDonald's, "or we could just stop at Cumby's," referring to a Cumberland Farms convenience store. When in college, she referred to Natural Ice, an inexpensive malt liquor that likes to get people arrested, by its more intimate name, "Natty Ice."

I was a useless older brother. I didn't do homework, so I couldn't help her with academics. When she ended up in the class of a high school teacher I had nearly driven insane several years earlier, she diplomatically pointed out that she and I were not actually blood relatives.

But when she got into serious trouble, she always ran to me, because she knew I had probably been in a far worse situation.

My sister always saw right through me, perhaps because once you've engaged in near-lethal physical combat with someone, you share a unique bond.

Our relationship had another benefit, for it allowed me to claim a certain level of worldliness, at least through association.

"Well, I'm not sure I know anything about this French Revolution you keep asking about, but my little sister is from Korea," I said to my history teacher one day, stroking my chin with an air of erudition. "Perhaps I could check with her and get back to you."

And Cassandra allowed me to finally make broad, sweeping generalizations about the people of the country from which she came.

"She's from Korea," I responded whenever friends asked why my sister and I looked so different. "Everyone there is pretty cool."

THEY MIGHT BE GIANTS

Bigfoot. Santa Claus. Dragons. Unicorns. Giants. The Tooth Fairy.

Eventually, most of our childhood deities vanish into the ether. We learn they never existed in the first place, and we usually take it surprisingly well.

"Oh, a key figure in the creation of my moral compass was merely an invention? The person who gave me presents if I told the truth was a lie. Okay, well off to school I go."

That's why I'm so infatuated with André the Giant. Because he is the rarest of things. He is a mythological creature in whom I believed in my youth. And unlike the Easter Bunny, my parents never had to sit me down and nervously explain to me that he never really existed.

Born André René Roussimoff, Andre had a real-life genetic condition called "giantism." The disease, which was named by a wildly imaginative scientist, caused him to grow, and grow, and grow until his heart gave out.

I will always be awed by his existence. I like to imagine meeting him at a restaurant for dinner, where his Brobding-nagian frame would cast a shadow across the entire room.

"That's just my friend, André," I'd tell frightened customers. "He has giantism. He's a giant."

From that point forward, people would half expect a fire-breathing dragon to swoop into the room and join our table.

"We'll need a table for three," I'd say nonchalantly to the hostess. "Our friend Harold will be joining us. He has dragonism. He's a dragon."

When I was a kid, the World Wrestling Federation, or WWF, was enormously popular. At the time in the mid-1980s the vast majority of children believed vehemently that they were watching real, brutal, unscripted combat between competitors who split their time between the ring, the tanning booth, the steroid trough and the traveling circus haberdasher.

But as my schoolmates engaged in heated debates about these wrestlers over our inedible lunchroom burgers, I was always a skeptic.

The Iron Sheik was not a sheik, I realized. The Undertaker was not really a huge, undead ghoul. Kilt-clad Rowdy Roddy Piper wasn't even Scottish; he was Canadian, a heritage that suggested he wasn't a fierce Highland freedom fighter, but rather an affable fellow with access to affordable prescriptions drugs.

Unlike those characters, André the Giant didn't use gimmicks or shticks. He didn't even wear bright colors or wave banners or flags. He wrestled in a simple black leotard that, while it was the size of a parachute, always seemed insufficient for the task of containing his girth.

He was strong as an ox, but he looked like he had never set foot in a gym. Like his strength was part of his soul; like an elemental aspect of his essence. Unlike everyone else, his skin was the color of pink human flesh, not shiny bronze.

He had fierce thickets of woolly muttonchops covering his immense cheeks. And he looked like the type of creature you might see munching on a whole goat, the way you or I enjoy a slice of pizza. Like someone French villagers would hire a knight to keep from gobbling up all their crops.

My classmates' ignorance went well beyond fake wrestling. They were authoritative and vocal about human biology, specifically procreation, government, and any other topic that came up.

Upperclassmen in particular—kids who went to the middle school and were sometimes spotted talking to girls without fainting—were viewed as wise sages. In retrospect, everything they ever taught me was laced with stunning inaccuracy.

Even grown-ups, I'm starting to realize, regularly misled me. So much of what I was told in those early years was later proven false.

Planets weren't actually planets. Healthy foods turned out to be bad for you, and vice versa. Movie stars and athletes who were once our idols all eventually died or fell from grace amid some awful scandal.

Now I'm starting to question my grasp on even the most basic knowledge.

As a child, I assumed seven billion adults were devoting the majority of their time and energy to my edification. They were, I thought, on earth primarily to answer my scattershot questions with clear, well-researched, completely unbiased answers.

As my daughter simultaneously gains the ability to speak English and open the door to whatever room I'm currently hiding in while I try to write, I'm realizing that might not have been the case.

In reality, most of my knowledge of the world around me was provided by people—my parents and teachers among them—who were merely throwing randomly generated words in my general direction in an attempt to fend me off. These were not scholars, carefully handing down generations of knowledge. They were weary men and women approaching middle age, a time when the impulse to discuss metaphysics is slowly usurped by an overwhelming need to drink coffee and talk about drywall. And they were being verbally assaulted by the most annoying thing in the world: a little boy.

At first, I bombarded them with questions that were mostly gibberish. Then words crept in. Then content.

"Doggy?"

"What's steam?"

"Who was Daniel Webster?"

"Does the blue color look blue to everyone?"

"How old is the oldest person in the world?"

"Is there a God, and if so, what type of hat does he wear?"

These questions were often directed at my mom while she tried to buckle a car seat, my dad while he operated a tractor, or my teacher while she tried to erase obscene drawings from the blackboard.

Their answers were given without thought. The trick for these adults was not the veracity of their words, but rather their quantity. Give the kid enough information and surely he'll shut up for a minute.

What I find truly terrifying is that everything they ever told me stuck. My brain soaked it all in. It's particularly surprising given the fact that you have to delve fairly deeply into the alphabet to locate the letters that populated most of my report cards. If you read between the lines on my teachers' written evaluations, you could see the places where they rubbed their temples, gazed out the window for a moment, and swallowed the desire to write the word "dullard" and be done with it.

But secretly, I was learning every fallacious thing I was told.

It is a problem that has manifested itself for years now. Every few weeks, I'll be discussing some issue on which I think I'm well informed.

"Oh look," I'll say as a Monarch butterfly wafts by. "A barn swallow!"

"Did you know," I'll explain with total confidence, "that Santa Claus is nearly 3000 years old?"

These moments are awkward even in one-on-one conversations. The awkwardness is amplified at dinner parties.

Once corrected, I struggle to understand how I could have been so misinformed for so long. Surely I didn't just make it up. Then I always remember some adult trying to maneuver through Massachusetts traffic and absentmindedly answering my questions without looking away from the road.

Now I'm guilty of it, too. I know, because I have on multiple occasions told my young daughter that "magic" is the scientific basis for things like barcode scanners and our microwave.

In the future, I'm going to try to be more careful. I'm going to stick to the facts whenever possible. It certainly doesn't have to make things boring.

At least I still get to look her in the eye and tell her that giants sometimes walk the earth.

MY BABY IS A PRINCESS

I wear a lot of khaki. It's a canvas upon which even the most banal stains take on a romantic hue. Splash coffee, beer and baby food on a white shirt, and you look like either a very simple slob or a very bad father. Those same stains on a khaki torso lead the mind down all sorts of exotic paths.

The ketchup splatter becomes blood from a poison-tipped Kalapalo arrow. Chocolate ice cream, which I dropped while trying to climb into my Kia Rio hatchback, turns into mud, smeared into the fabric during a brawl with a Portuguese slave-trader. A slight tear in the back, created when I tried to crawl under my desk to retrieve an elusive pen, might show just how close a snow leopard came to eating me for lunch on some faraway mountaintop.

I like to think my clothes add a dash of excitement to everyone's day. When people see me reading intently about the absorbent qualities of different diapers at the grocery store, I want them to suspect I might, at any moment, toss them to the ground and exclaim: "Forget this. I'm going on an African safari."

My wife tries to rob my wardrobe of this romance.

"My husband," she likes to tell people, "wears a lot of brown."

It wasn't always this way. I spent my teen years during the glory days of grunge, when teenagers around the world showed their disdain for societal norms by scouring thrift shops for flannels outgrown by obese lumberjacks and cardigan sweaters in which somebody's grandmother had recently died.

As a teenager, I was under the mistaken impression people actually cared how I dressed. As I grew up, I gradually realized nothing could be further from the truth. All it takes is a short walk down any street in the United States to see adults, even ones with jobs and families, are happy to go about their daily routines looking absolutely ridiculous.

That's why, whenever I see a high school student who looks like Dracula or the Joker, I think: "Good for him. He gets it."

When I arrived at college, I owned exactly enough things to fill one backpack. This, combined with the fact that these were things leftover from my grunge phase, made me look unambiguously shiftless in affluent Saint Augustine, Florida.

Surrounded by college freshmen who drove Nissan Xterras and used magical plastic cards to pay for things, I was something of an enigma.

"Are you... poor?" my friends would ask.

"I don't think so," I'd answer, gnawing on someone else's Hungry Howie's pizza crust for dinner. "Can one be poor and fat at the same time?"

While they drove around on the beaches, I worked in bakeries and hardware stores, eventually earning enough money to try the other end of the pizza.

People pitied me until the day, my skin bronzed by the sun and a thicket of black hair extending my jawline, I first put on some khaki.

Whispers about my station in life were immediately replaced by awed murmurs: "That's Matt Geiger," they said as I walked home after a Saturday morning of making blueberry muffins for minimum wage. "He's rugged and independent. I heard he just got back from an adventure. He doesn't even want a car—he just walks everywhere, carrying everything he owns in that backpack."

"He is," they concluded, "an adventurer."

It was a far cry from my early childhood, when my mother, possibly still angry at me for nauseating her for nine months, decided to dress me exactly like Christopher Robin, the foppish little English boy who palled around with Winnie the Pooh. Gussied up in fancy shoes, short shorts and socks that almost reached my sweater vest, I might as well have been wearing a bullseye.

Even today, I can't look at childhood pictures of myself without getting a strong desire to beat myself up and take my lunch money.

"Won't you please bully me, kind sir?" is what those early outfits said to my peers.

If my young daughter's wardrobe could speak, it would say something very different. Probably something along the lines of: "My parents are dressing me exclusively in hand-me-down clothes provided by oddly-shaped toddlers and new garments gifted by colorblind grandparents."

On the rare occasions we go shopping for new clothes for Hadley, we are confronted with only two options.

The first is clothing designed to sexualize infants. Pants that say: "Juicy" across the rump, or shirts that feature glittering dollar signs on the chest.

While this offends me as a father, I also tend to think, "Good luck." It's hard enough for well behaved people to find love. I can't imagine someone who still poops in her pants at the dinner table meeting with great success on the dating scene.

The rest of the outfits for young girls all fall into the "princess" category.

I suspect King George III would delight in the fact that, more than two centuries after our nation shed so much blood to rid ourselves of a king and queen, we still desperately want to be part of a monarchy. The catch being that we all want to live only in a kingdom in which we are the royalty.

I don't sense any irony in this reverence, which is really no different than worshiping any other form of fascist dictator.

Surely I would encounter some scowls if I started dressing my daughter up like Pol Pot. But dressing her up as a princess? That's perfectly fine, apparently.

It doesn't really matter anyway. Soon she'll be able to pick out her own outfits. She even walks sometimes.

It's a prospect I find particularly exciting. Walking down the street, a khaki-clad explorer and a little girl dressed like Princess Elsa or Fidel Castro.

I hope when people see us, they think: "Look at them. They must be going on an adventure together."

MONKHOOD

I wanted to be a monk. Brimming with mirth, a crooked tonsure atop by head. My earthy cloak secured by a length of rustic rope and strained by a belly full of warm pretzels and frothy ale.

I pictured myself standing in the entrance to an ancient monastery. Behind me, the light from a fire would perform a gleeful jig on dank stone walls. At my side, a brawny, ursine, brown-and-white dog would stand. Together, we would gaze out at a frigid, windswept mountain range, the vastness of which reminded us of the universe's endless mysteries.

It was largely an aesthetic desire. I liked the idea of wearing a single article of clothing—a robe—every day. Yet recent personal experience had taught me that wearing a robe—in this case a bathrobe—all day in secular life invites people to call you "lazy" and "slovenly."

My winters would be spent studying texts. Copying gilded illustrations from decaying calfskin pages originally adorned by earlier monks who surely lived in a cave, on some remote island.

My summers would be spent growing medicinal herbs, or perhaps wandering through mountain passes, pausing frequently to lean on my staff, smiling and nodding as I slowly, surely figured out the meaning of life.

I had a professor who was a former Franciscan monk. I visited his office frequently to engage in reconnaissance. Sitting at his desk and playing with a Jesus Christ action figure he turned to when in need of a chuckle, he provided glimpses into life in a monastery.

I thought I would make an excellent monk. I was already studying philosophical and theological texts, so that part would be a piece of cake. If I could fake it in college, I could fake it in a monastery.

I began reading about the various religious orders. My first criterion, of course, was the robes. They had to be of the Friar Tuck variety. Brown and baggy. Leaving room for the spiritual and physical growth that would inevitably accompany a life spent reading and eating cave-aged cheese. A shade of brown capable of masking any stain.

Most of the modern vestments didn't provide the vibe I was going for. I liked the Buddhists' beliefs, but I know men of my girth should not drape themselves in bright orange. Only earth tones would do for this future holy man.

The Dominicans' black and white wasn't rugged enough. I thought the Knights Templar looked pretty good in their white and red, but the fact that they ceased to exist in the Middle Ages made joining their ranks difficult.

I wanted, I realized but did not say aloud, to look like a Jedi.

"So, what type of staff did you get?" I asked my professor while exiting class one day. "Was it tall and gnarled? Did you guys have beards, or were you clean shaven? Did you wear sandals, or does footwear not matter, since your shoes are hidden underneath your robes?"

But my journey to monkhood was also fraught with worries. As I learned more about the inner workings of various monasteries, I noticed a lot of things you weren't allowed to do.

A vow of poverty would be fine, being as it was essentially just a verbal affirmation of my current situation. But most of the other vows seemed a bit harsh for my taste.

I've never really liked the idea of being defined by a long list of things I've promised not to do.

Rasputin, the Siberian "mad monk" who left a trail of debauchery in his wake, offered some encouragement. Having once read a biographer refer to his morning prayers as "well earned," I saw him as an inspiration.

But deeper digging revealed he wasn't actually a real, ordained monk. Plus, he was shot, stabbed, poisoned, drowned and frozen, all of which are occupational hazards I find hard to accept.

My professor tried to dissuade me. He even suggested I didn't know what the word "monk" meant.

When I asked him if he learned any cool spells behind the walls of his monastery, he cocked his head to the side and looked at me quizzically: "You know we're not wizards, right?"

"I know, Dr. Thompson," I replied. "I'm not an idiot. Do you get a wand right away when you join, or does that happen later?"

And soon enough, the dream dissipated. Life went on, and I forgot all about my plan. My closet remained full of shirts and pants, and I never promised not to do anything.

But from time to time, I still find myself thinking about religion, and religious men and women. After all, you can't study religion without studying people.

The question I like most is not: "Does your God exist?" After all, that's a question without an answer, at least not in this world.

A far more interesting question, I think, is: "What is your God like?"

After all, you can tell a lot about people by meeting their deity.

Perhaps because I still think about these things, I'm becoming a bit monkish these days. I have a wife and a daughter, which I understand is frowned upon within the walls of most monasteries. But I also have a massive brown and white dog. If I ever want a big pretzel and some local ale, I just walk over to The Grumpy Troll, a little brewery in the town where I live. I'm getting a nice little bald spot on top of my head, as if the Universe wants me to have a stylish tonsure. I have a fireplace, and I still like to flip through old philosophical and theological texts.

Sometimes I even stand in the doorway, feeling the flames at my back and gazing out into the wintery vastness of the American Midwest. If you ever see my silhouette, bathrobe draped around me, big dog at my side, rest assured I'm quietly giving thanks for all the mysteries the Universe has given us to ponder.

MY BABY KILLED MY CAT

Peter was a lazy, mercurial presence in our house. Even in his old age, he stuck to a rigorous daily routine that included sleeping wherever I wanted to sit, and distributing a layer of hair, like little strands of poison ivy, all over everything. He also savagely attacked people foolish enough to think a purring, prostrated feline didn't mean them any harm. And of course, he liked to vomit dramatically whenever we tried to eat dinner or entertain guests.

Whenever my wife has questioned my devotion to her, I've always been quick to point out that my love for her is so strong it compelled me to take in and live alongside what was essentially a wild animal.

At 25 pounds, Peter the cat was the equivalent of a feral wolverine living in our home. I often imagined how silly we must have looked, taking the long route through the house to avoid him when he was in a bad temper, or leaping out of the way when he jumped up onto the couch next to us. It is remarkable what you can get used to in your own house.

After an attack, I always felt like the neighbor of a serial killer, being interviewed on the evening news.

"He just seemed perfectly normal," I would think. "I never would have suspected he was planning to kill and eat me."

No amount of menace on my part, pleading from my wife, or growling from the dog could ever daunt Peter. His only real fear was plastic bags, which to him sounded uncannily like the ferocious thrumming of the hooves of the horses of the Apocalypse.

When we brought our infant daughter home, we stocked up on hydrogen peroxide and showed her, with much trepidation and a lot of protective hand waving, the cat we assumed would teach her a few puzzling, bloody lessons about animal behavior.

We could never figure out Peter's rules for non-engagement. It was as if he occasionally signed a peace treaty, but refused to inform us of the hundreds of rules and conditions contained within it.

"Oh, Matt's wearing a blue shirt today," the cat would think. "Now I have to kill him."

There was no mistaking his feelings as he gazed into our daughter's eyes for the first time. The entire living situation, he felt, had grown instantly and completely unbearable.

"There is no way," he was thinking, "I am going to live with that horrible little creature."

And he didn't. He quickly died of what the vet said was old age, but what I am fairly certain was a fatal case of feline scorn.

When I noticed he felt unwell, I picked him up and drove him to the vet. When I walked in and placed him on the examination table, the doctor did the things doctors do—listening to his heart, checking his breathing, and feeling around to see if organs were doing anything alarming.

"I'm sorry to tell you," said the vet. "He's going to die."

"Yep," I replied casually, always willing to chat philosophically about life and death. "I know he's pretty old. He won't be around forever. I mean, none of us will, right?"

"Um, I mean," interjected the vet with a certain urgency that made me stop gazing at a painting on the wall. "Right now. I'm very sorry."

Not as sorry, I thought, as I would be when I returned home to my wife—a mere 15 minutes after leaving the house—without a cat.

While writing this, I toyed with ending on some kind of high note. Searching the recesses of my brain for a memory of the cat acting tenderly, or showing love or affection. But such passages would be an unfitting epilogue for the creature with whom I lived for so many years.

I will say this: These days, whenever I walk around a corner and nothing tries to assassinate me. Whenever I sit down to watch a movie and don't instantly feel my skin begin to itch. Whenever I take the shortest route from one room to another, because I'm not afraid of having my leg eviscerated, I feel like my world is slightly less exciting. And that's not a good thing.

I frequently like to slightly misquote the great Oscar Wilde, stating, "It is absurd to divide people into good and bad. People are either interesting or boring."

Peter was never, ever boring. And for that he is missed. Luckily, we have some scars by which to remember him.

THE ANTI-FEMINIST
AND THE CHILD

Socrates said: "I know that I know nothing." It was a claim that famously made him the wisest man in all of Greece, because he at least knew one more thing than everyone else.

My first philosophy professor knew quite a bit. She was a lean, jagged woman, with spectacular long hair, worn like a frizzy cape the color of a traffic safety cone.

She was, she explained to us, an "anti-feminist." In multiple books with vaguely bawdy titles, she argued that modern feminism was based on the presumption that women are inferior and must therefore be coddled. One was called *Feminism Under Fire*. Another, called *Undressing Feminism*, featured a sultry photo of her on the cover, her white dress being removed by a pair of bodiless male hands.

She was, I thought, sending some very mixed messages. "Is she trying to kill feminism, or seduce it?" I whispered to one of my classmates.

We heard rumors she could do one-handed pushups. That she traveled mysteriously to the Middle East to consult various government agencies on the nuances of what is or is not torture. Given the draconian nature of her tests, it seemed safe to assume she was a pretty enthusiastic proponent of waterboarding.

To her, scoffing around stupidity was unavoidable—like sneezing near pollen or crying in close proximity to onions. It was just something that happened in a world populated by the dull.

Sometimes she would gather up her hair, with masochistic aggression that suggested it had been misbehaving, and swirl it into some kind of leaning tower on top of her head, inexplicably holding it together with something I could have sworn was a chopstick. As someone who has trouble using chopsticks for their intended purpose, I had never dared consider branching out and trying nonconventional applications.

One morning in logic class, she told us about a recent date. Her suitor had consumed ten beers and a few oysters through the course of the evening. When he grew ill, he proclaimed to her: "I'm never eating oysters again."

"I won't be seeing him again," she barked. "Anyone who struggles so mightily with causation strikes out with this woman."

She was someone who argued vehemently against the existence of God, then—just to confuse us, we figured—started dating a Catholic guy and mentioned she might be converting.

She had a habit of asking "why" over and over again, until you inevitably entered treacherous intellectual territory. That one word, uttered over and over, has the power to unhinge even the brightest student, because eventually everyone's well of knowledge runs dry.

At the end of every debate with her, young men and women all said the same thing: "I really have no idea."

She would smirk, pleased that she had taught us something.

One morning, a student in our logic class collapsed and lost consciousness. I was worried about him, but also suspected him of doing it as a desperate, ultimately successful attempt to get out of taking that morning's impossible quiz.

"Why," I admonished myself as medics rolled him away, "didn't I think of that!"

We were shaken, but vaguely comforted by the fact that there was absolutely no way our professor would make us finish the pop quiz while we could still hear sirens.

But we had forgotten, this was someone who had probably watched people get electrocuted with car batteries during "interrogations" in hot, sandy rooms.

We at least had air conditioning, she thought. *We were wimps.*

"I'm sure that frightened many of you," she said magnanimously as the medics headed down the hallway and the door to our classroom closed. "I want to be fair, so I won't count that time against you and you can have until 10:15 to finish."

I have a hunch she made a trip to the hospital after class ended that day, just to bring that poor guy the test. It would have been fitting for her to hand it to him, like a bouquet of flowers, then sit by the edge of the bed with a stopwatch. "I want to be fair," she'd say. "So if you lose consciousness, I won't count that time against you."

I was also in her classroom on September 11, 2001. While most other teachers simply gave up on the day, letting the terrorists win, I guess, she sat us down for a very lively debate about ethics and religion, foreign policy and social norms.

"This," she explained as we heard bizarre reports of planes crashing into buildings, "is why we study philosophy. This is why we ask the questions we ask."

One autumn, I left college for a week and headed home to Massachusetts. My mom dragged me to some kind of party—an assemblage of people who frowned upon interesting conversation.

I was standing on the outskirts of the event to avoid the usual line of interrogation from adults: "You're majoring in philosophy? What type of job will that get you? How much do philosophers get paid these days?"

It wasn't their snark that stung—it was the fact that they were asking me what amounted to rhetorical questions. They knew the answers, but they wanted to hear me say them aloud: "Yes. None. Not much."

While hiding, I stumbled across a little boy. He was like a toddler, but slightly less wobbly in stance and verbiage.

"So," I began. "What's your name?"

"Gus," he replied.

I asked all the questions adults are expected to ask when making conversation, doing my best impersonation of the people who liked to accost me. Where did he live? Did he go to school yet? What did his parents do? Was he enjoying the holidays? Did he know how hard it was to find a job with a bachelor's degree in philosophy?

He answered most questions with a shrug, as if I were asking him how to keep a soufflé from deflating or how many years we had until the sun burned out.

"I'm only five," he eventually said. "I don't know much."

"Fair enough," I said. "You just might be the smartest person here."

He shrugged again and galloped away.

Today, when people ask me my views on politics or parenting, on the environment or gun laws, I take a page from my friend, Gus, who was the wisest man in Massachusetts one day, many years ago.

"I'm middle-aged," I tell people. "I don't know much."

RAISED BY WOLVES

One of my friends was raised by wolves, and he turned out just fine.

So why, if he became a contributing member of society, does everyone fret about parenting?

Scaring people into thinking they need a variety of guidebooks and special devices to raise a child to adulthood is a multi-billion dollar industry these days. Car seats, like reduced-price fish, expire before you can even get them home. Small children seem to be singlehandedly holding up the entire North American buckle industry, and everything we own comes with straps and snaps intended to secure a person who can't even do a sit-up.

When used according to the manufacturers' instructions, they make my angelic infant daughter look vaguely like Hannibal Lecter. I see people eying her with the nervous glances you give to a large dog in a muzzle.

"Surely," they think to themselves as they look at the maze of restraints, "she must be capable of terrible things if they have to keep her manacled like that."

Somewhat surprisingly given how lucrative this racket seems to be, the child-rearing accessories have been rolling in for free these days.

It started long before I ever met my daughter, and it continued mercilessly, like some kind of perverse Christmas morning when you have no idea what most of your presents are, even after you open them.

By the time little Hadley came home from the hospital, my wife and I looked like we had spent the prior nine months packing for a dangerous, complicated voyage into a perilous, uncharted region. Like Shackleton headed to the Antarctic, we lumbered around slowly, weighed down by hundreds of pounds of gear and the expectation that we might die of exposure or get eaten by a bear. I half expected someone to give us a Sherpa at the baby shower.

Everything comes with a series of warnings on it. One of the most prevalent is: "Never leave a child unattended."

While it's sound advice, it has been slapped by people with no sense of irony onto a series of seats, swings and toys that are clearly specifically designed to occupy your child while you do something else.

We were given conflicting parenting books, which led me to consistently fail the Scott Fitzgerald IQ exam. ("The test of a first-rate intelligence is the ability to hold two opposing ideas in mind at the same time and still retain the ability to function.")

According to these books, my daughter must be vaccinated or she will perish. Also, vaccinations will probably kill her. Soothing her when she's upset will rob her of the ability to self-soothe, and leaving her alone when she bawls will turn her into a raving sociopath.

The books are at least superior to the Internet, which is essentially a vast repository of incorrect, hysterical "facts" designed for people who enjoy the coexistent states of self-righteousness and resolute inaccuracy. (This stands in stark contrast to the Internet's stellar reputation as a forum for intelligent, measured debate about issues of politics and religion.)

The first time my baby spit up, I googled it. A series of deranged, though apparently sincere parents informed me this was surely the symptom of several fatal diseases. Or it meant she had eaten too much. Or maybe eaten too little. In one thing they were all in agreement: I had failed as a father, and my baby was very sick.

I later learned in spectacular fashion from my daughter, the difference between "spitting up" and "throwing up," which have about as much in common as a uncorking a bottle of champagne and detonating a hydrogen bomb.

The Internet caused me, in those early, blurry days and sleepless nights, to worry about the following problems and ailments: pooping too much, not pooping enough, crying too much, not crying enough, sleeping too much, not sleeping enough. The list goes on.

My favorite thread on the Internet was started by the following question, posted by a parent who was probably on the verge of tears: "My dog just licked my baby. *WHAT SHOULD I DO*?"

I'll admit that my friend, whose family owns a wolf sanctuary in Ipswich, Massachusetts, had some guidance from his human parents, but his success as a person proves you probably don't have to worry too much when your baby gets licked by a dog, or even a wolf.

The best advice I received came from friends. It was simple and consistent. "Feed her. Stay off the Internet," they said. "You'll figure out the rest as you go."

And that seems to be the way things are headed.

It's pretty clear I'm not the leader on this expedition, anyway. Nor is my wife. Hadley is the one leading us on whatever voyage, to whatever far off, uncharted land this is. I'm just a pack animal, or maybe, on my good days, the cook. I hope we don't get icebound and have to resort to cannibalism, but fear isn't the primary emotion at work here. It's the excitement that comes with an unknown destination. And my little captain, dressed like Hannibal Lecter and leading like Shackleton, is clearly at the helm. She has the compass, and the ability to go wherever she wants. I'm just here to help her get there.

THE OLD LADY WHO LIVED
IN A CHICKEN COOP

The best friend I ever had was an old lady who lived in a chicken coop.

She wore black, cat-eye glasses, peacock-blue dresses and earth-colored pantyhose. She used pink, plastic rollers to style her gray hair, covering her head under a crinkly, clear plastic bag whenever the sky insinuated drizzle.

She lived next door, a built-in babysitter for my parents when they moved into our farmhouse. Her home had been converted, at some point, into a human dwelling, but its bones were still those of a henhouse.

Much of my childhood was spent sitting on her vast lap, positioned next to whatever she was knitting for me or reading to me. She spoke in a sing-song New England accent.

One winter, she made for me a wool cap, stitching the name "Mathew" onto the brow.

"My name is with two Ts," I told her when it was done, using a lack of tact specialized in by young boys.

She smiled, said "Oh," and disappeared into the closet to retrieve a ball of yarn. A few days later she handed me a new hat. It said "Matthew" on the front.

I thought she was going to call child services on my dad when he told me the truth about Santa Claus.

She let me stay up late each night, until the conclusion of that evening's Boston Red Sox game, even if the innings stretched on and on. She scored each game, with a pencil and little red notebook, keeping what I always did and still do consider the official record of every at-bat.

She had to put a special, plastic heightener on her toilet so she wouldn't get stuck. She called it, with a glimmer in her eye, her "throne."

She took in a black barn cat who used to perch on her lap and kneed her meaty legs like bread dough. That cat could do no wrong, even when he gave her a staph infection that nearly killed her.

She allowed me to play Batman on her roof, despite the fairly obvious damage my grappling hook did to the chimney. She let me eat carrots, still dusted with soil, right out of a garden that was slightly shaded by sunflowers.

She was there when I got into my first brawl. I was a toddler, innocently playing on the front lawn, when a big brute of a boy, with an ugly snout, a muscular jaw, and the not irrelevant advantage of having a lawyer for a father, tottered over and bit down on my shoulder.

He proceeded to make little growling, vaguely pit-bull-ish noises as I tried desperately to flee.

I didn't yet know how to dress myself, read or even properly use a toilet 100 percent of the time, but even I knew it was rude to bite people. It wasn't like knowing which fork to use for your salad or how to write a cursive "r." This was a basic concept that had been mastered even by the family dog, Boomer, whose favorite mental exercises included rolling in cow manure and eating mid-sized rocks.

When the adults finally pried him off of me, blood was streaming down my arm and the flesh around the wound was a medley of yellow and purple.

"He's going through a biting phase," explained his yuppie mother, employing the same casual tone people today use to explain they are "doing the gluten-free thing."

When I was about 11, my best friend began a gradual transformation. Her chubby face grew gaunt, her skin jaundiced, and her eyes a little wetter than before. I stopped going to visit, even actively avoiding her when our paths crossed.

When my mother asked why I never visited her anymore, I said it was because I knew she was going to die. I don't recall if this was my first existential realization of mortality, that philosophical gut-punch. Or maybe I was just worried that she would drop dead in front of me and I would somehow catch the blame. This had happened before once, with a hamster, and I knew I was not particularly good at explaining away dead bodies. One day, she asked my mother to give her a ride to the hospital. She had a nice ensemble, complete with a fresh, peacock-blue dress, in her top drawer. She asked my mom to fetch it for her, calling it her "going away" outfit.

She lay for a little while, seemingly melting into the hospital bed. My parents pulled me out of school to say goodbye.

I remember standing awkwardly in the little room, happy to have gotten out of class early, but disappointed by the fact that Nathan, my nemesis on the playground, was so robust while she was left to perish.

I remember she called me over, told me one thing—it's something I'll leave between the two of us—and let me go.

When she died, I didn't feel particularly sad. Just lonely.

Last week, I received a package in the mail. It included an assortment of old, childhood possessions. At the bottom of the box, carefully sealed inside a plastic bag, was an old, red-and-white notebook.

"What's this?" I wondered as I opened it up. On the first page, in faded pencil, was the box score from a July 3 game between the Boston Red Sox and the Toronto Blue Jays. The Red Sox lost, 3-2. Dwight Evans had a pretty good day and Wade Boggs, as usual, had a hit.

At the very bottom of the page was a note, written in a serene hand. It was the spot where she always jotted down the most important thing about each game. It was three words: "Watched with Matthew."

"YOU ARE VERY FAT"

I used to trade English words for Chinese food.

It was a good deal, even though they didn't understand all my words, and I couldn't identify most of what I ate. It was also preferable to the opposite, since no sane person would willingly trade anything for English food.

It all started when I walked past a Chinese restaurant with a sign in the window.

"ENGLISH TEACHER WANTED," it stated.

"I speak English," I thought as I opened the door, "and I can think of no reason to withhold this knowledge from others."

I'd seen a lot of movies about this type of thing. My impression was that all you had to do was be white, show up and start speaking English to people. Eventually, I figured, your students begin to understand you through some kind of linguistic osmosis.

For a brief, selfish moment, I did consider hoarding all the words for myself.

But I quickly realized language is one of the few things you can give to someone without depleting your own stock of it. Give someone food or money, and you'll wind up with less. Not words. They are like some mythological snake that will grow to the size of its cage.

All you have to do is give them a bigger cage.

I expected the kid would be troubled, probably from an inner city somewhere, and that I could impart folksy life lessons on her. In return, she'd teach me some unexpected lesson about kindness or charity. Like I said, I've seen the movie a thousand times.

The problem, I soon realized, is that in the real world, if someone doesn't speak your language, it doesn't really matter how heartily you pummel them with words. It's like playing charades with a blind person; extra flamboyant hand gestures aren't going to get the job done.

When I first walked in, I announced my benevolence in ornate fashion. It was probably too ostentatious, even for native English speakers.

Greeted with perplexed, quizzical faces, I toned it down and tried again.

It was still too much.

A white-apron-clad, middle-aged man behind the counter handed me a menu and pointed to the numbers that accompanied each meal. "Which number?" he coaxed.

They thought I was extraordinarily bad at ordering. I tried several more times, each time boiling my words down to be more simple, rustic and masculine. I started to feel like Ernest Hemingway.

Eventually I ended up sitting in a chilly corner booth with a young student. I'll call her Jennifer here to protect her anonymity.

Not surprisingly, her Mandarin was proving fairly useless in her Wisconsin elementary school classroom.

She seemed to grasp humor in English before she was comfortable with the more mundane aspects of the language. The result was that while she couldn't yet read the word "the," she could say all sorts of whimsical things in a tiny, but nonetheless bombastic, soprano.

It was problematic at times, this learning style. When she pointed at me one day and stated: "You are very fat," my first instinct was not to laud her. But this was a child just beginning to pick up the basics of English, and she had strung together a perfect sentence.

"Excellent," I said, clapping my hands and grimacing. "Yes. Yes, I am."

"And your shirts all have many coffee stains on them," she added with a hint of erudition.

"Uh, well, yes," I replied. "Let's stop freelancing now and go back to talking about this kid in your school book."

"You have crumbs of food in your beard…" she continued.

The problem with the primers she was supposed to study was that they included scenarios and people who do not exist in English, nor in any other language. Kids interacted exclusively with mail carriers and firefighters, and their lives had a very vague, generic quality to them. They came from a poorly drawn society in which technology had lagged behind, stuck amidst the landline telephones and boom box radios of the 1980s. Balloons were ubiquitous, yet no one had a cell phone.

Plus, as someone who writes thousands of words each day for multiple publications, it was disheartening to realize these authors were being paid so much more, per word, than I was.

Tutoring began in one of two ways. I would arrive early and wait for the school bus to drop her off, or I would show up late and Jennifer would emerge from the cubbyhole beneath the cash register where she liked to nap after school.

She and her mother always asked the same question when they first saw me.

"You and your wife have baby yet?" they'd say hopefully.

"No," I smiled, "no baby."

"Aww," they would reply, shaking their heads with disappointment that transcended language.

They seemed to think everyone was always actively trying to progenerate, which could not have been further from the truth in my case. I liked my money and my free time, so I wasn't trying to have a kid. It's the same reason people who like jogging don't go out and actively try to contract polio.

Next, they would bring me a menu — not the American-ized one full of syrupy sauces doused over deep-fried hunks of meat—but rather the document they offered to people from China. I would gaze at it for a few moments, puzzled by items such as "small fishes" and "not chicken," then point to something at random.

Jennifer's mother would smile, shake her head and say "no" while taking the menu away. "This," she'd add, pointing to something completely different. "You eat this."

We must have looked odd, a waifish child with hair so black it looked purple, wearing a pink *Hello Kitty* coat to stay warm in the chilly corner booth, and a 32-year-old white guy with crumbs in his beard, chowing down together on sticky, glutinous treats and indistinguishable dried fruits.

There were little meat pies wrapped in rice-based dough and steamed to rubbery perfection. There were special cakes for certain days of the year, or so I gathered from the way her mom pointed to the calendar while plopping them down on the table in front of me.

I could identify rice and noodles, but the stuff in between looked like an impressionist painter's take on the ingredients in my refrigerator at home. Their imitation meats were so meat-like that I was left to assume each was simply one kind of animal flesh imitating another.

Tutoring was an enjoyable experience. Reading terrible books, eating mysterious food, and pretending to converse with people who speak a different language are all fun on their own. Put them together, and you have a nice hour.

I eventually stopped going. I had more responsibilities at work, and I had trouble finding the time to sit in the corner booth with Jennifer. Plus, her English was improving so rapidly that I wondered whether my help was still adequate. Her questions became more nuanced, and she grew tired of my usual response when I wasn't sure how to answer: "Let's look it up in the *Associated Press Style Guide.*"

I saw her mother several years later. She was watching Jennifer's new little brother as he romped on the playground.

"You have baby yet?" she asked.

HOMELAND SECURITY

When you work at a bookstore in a shopping mall in New Jersey, there is only one productive way to pass the time. You flip through the inventory, searching for characters with interesting jobs.

Hopefully, you think to yourself as the belligerent olfactory cacophony of the food court gropes your clothing, you can find a character with a more interesting job than this one. Then you can go get such a job, and never again set foot in a national retail chain that, due to what I assume was a significant and costly clerical error, made the mistaken assumption that the people of New Jersey have an insatiable appetite for literature.

Nearly every job I came across seemed alluring by comparison.

Skimming the pages of Hemingway, I considered becoming a drunk. "But that's really more of a hobby than a profession," I realized, placing *The Sun Also Rises* back on an end cap. "I need a paycheck."

Picking up a copy of Dostoyevsky's *Crime and Punishment*, I read a bit about the protagonist, Raskolnikov. "Well, I could be a murderer," I thought as I read. But if I worked in the mall for much longer, that was going to happen organically. Plus, Raskolnikov's fever dreams seemed like more than I could handle.

Then I headed to the children's section. I hoped those books would provide some bright, colorful, large-fonted guidance. But they were focused solely on four professions, and I didn't want to be a police officer, firefighter, teacher or crossing guard.

Visiting the children's section was always an adventure, because teenagers liked to take lurid adult magazines from a rack in the front of the store and hide them within the pages of the picture books for kids. Our primary responsibility as employees was to locate and remove these magazines to avoid very awkward confrontations with angry parents.

The bookstore also had a depressing, Jim-Crow-era feel to it. Books by black authors or about black characters were relegated to their own section. A little sign, titled "African American," hung over these shelves, giving them a bizarre, 1960s Alabama water fountain quality that made all of us squirm.

It seemed like books, a medium where you can't even see the writer or the characters, would be a perfect art form in which to escape from the trappings of race, but this store clearly felt differently.

I envisioned some executive, sitting in a boardroom somewhere, worrying about the mixing of black and white books. "It's not like the African American sections will be any worse than the rest of the store," he would explain to some timorous intern. "Just separate. I mean, we have to do this or else we might end up with a book about a white woman next to one about a black man."

One of my favorite things to do, when not searching for a new job in the inventory, was watch the handful of daily customers. They entered and hustled to the "Classic

Literature" section, where they would stand for a few moments like a little kid sentenced to a time out. They'd stare blankly at the books, stealing glances at their cell phones. Then, when they thought no one was looking, they'd scramble to their real destinations.

I think 90 percent of our sales were trashy romance novels and their even more brazen counterparts, the aforementioned adult magazines. And manga, which is kind of a genuine art form but also kind of just books that read right to left, about young, female protagonists who live alongside assorted robots and small, fluffy, flying animals.

When applying for the job, I thought my affection for reading was an asset. But that's like applying for a job at a restaurant and putting "I'm obese; it'll be great!" on your application.

Our value as employees was judged almost solely based on a single statistic. It was called "UPT," which stands for "Units Per Transaction." The idea was simple. They couldn't make enough money selling one book at a time, so they encouraged workers to sell multiple novels or magazines to every customer. The computers didn't take into account the nature or value of these items, however, so I exploited a pretty glaring hole. Near the cash register sat a box of chocolates and a stack of bookmarks. They cost mere cents.

"Would you mind buying a couple chocolates and a bookmark?" I asked customers. "We're judged here based on how many items we sell to each customer, and it would really help me out. I have a degree in philosophy, so if I lose this job there's a pretty good chance I'll remain unemployed, starve to death and stop existing. Then all my knowledge about the nature of existence will become even more useless than it is now, which would be unfortunate."

Shannon, my boss, had a mop of short red hair, a closet full of thick, broad-shouldered sweaters, and a penchant for making authoritative, spurious statements about literary matters.

"Most people mispronounce 'Pulitzer,'" she'd say to a customer she had ambushed on his way to the magazines. "It's supposed to be pronounced, 'Plutytzer.'"

"William Faulker," she'd mention to someone by the classics, "always put a leaf of basil in his mint juleps."

While flipping through *The Adventures of Sherlock Holmes*, I discovered a profession with promise. "That's it," I thought. "I'll become a private detective."

When that didn't pan out, I applied for a job as a security guard. I considered it a kind of glamorous, preemptive detective work. I would be like a sleuth in the "Future Crimes Unit" of a science fiction novel.

"With a good security guard, stuff doesn't even get stolen in the first place," I explained to myself. "With more good security guards around, the entire detecting industry would become obsolete. I'm on the cutting edge here."

My excitement diminished significantly when I received my uniform. In the brochure, the guards wore cool looking outfits that had an authoritarian, military appearance. But the real uniform was clearly made in a factory that cranked out Halloween costumes each fall.

A striking nylon affair, it had a thread count in the single digits and you could see through it if you held it up to a dim light. The tie was a clip-on, the badge was plastic, and the entire ensemble was the itchy-clothing equivalent of a movie set—just real enough to fool people from the right angle, but all hollow and vacant if looked at in the wrong lighting.

"You know what," I said to the boss. "You can keep it. I have to go to the library and look through some more books. Eventually I'll find the right profession."

RETURN OF THE NATIVITY

Every December in Alabama, well-intentioned Christians shout their faith to the world by placing garish, hollow plastic statues atop the bed of fallen pecans in the front yard.

The colors vary, but they can all be described using prefixes like "acid-" and "nuclear-." An acid-green Joseph prostrates himself next to a nuclear-blue Mary, gazing with polyethylene eyes at two of the three canonical wise men in this well-known biblical scene. (There are two, rather than three, because one has always either been made off with by neighborhood hooligans, or destroyed by a heathen dog.)

In really special nativity scenes, a searing-brown camel will stand nearby, motionlessly chewing her cud next to a neon-gray donkey.

For reasons that I think are pretty clear in the preceding description, the nativity scene never really garnered my affection in my early years. Primarily, I knew of these little displays as inoffensive, slightly comical little holiday sites that morons—including atheists and Christians alike— seemed to enjoy fighting over whenever they wound up too close to a town hall or a school building.

I was very different, in this regard and in many others, from the father of my college girlfriend. You may remember Mark, the fairly deaf engineer, who was kind enough to let me spend many holidays with him in the American South. This round man (not fat, just round), whom you met in a story I once wrote about Thanksgiving, loved his faith and therefore all things related to it, including plastic statues.

His voice cracking with the affability it always did when he grew excited, he spent much of his time over the holidays reciting a single mantra: "Jesus is the reason for the season."

It was a phrase he said when the issue came up, but also whenever there happened to be a lull in the conversation.

When asked if he would pick up some toilet paper when he headed to the store later, he might assume a puzzled expression, smile as he accepted the fact that he couldn't decipher what had been asked of him, and offer a friendly, gentle pat on the back: "Well, Jesus is the reason for the season."

Each year, Mark would ask his children, his friends, and anyone who happened to meander into his line of sight, if they would like to help him set up his nativity display.

While his deafness wasn't contagious, you would have thought it was whenever the subject was broached. People appeared to suddenly lose the ability to hear a man standing a few feet away. That, or they would suddenly develop superhuman hearing and run off in feigned response to some far-away call for help.

So each year, as the holiday drew near, Mark would eventually do it by himself. He'd head into the garage, pushing aside deflated soccer balls and jars of jam that had been boiled during the Ford administration, and haul out those religious figures.

Through the years they grew dusty and scuffed, somehow without becoming any less gaudy. He would build the stable, carefully laying down the straw all around, placing each piece carefully lest his little, plastic God be uncomfortable in his resting place. He would then connect several furlongs of extension cords together in an effort to test the capabilities of the little town's power grid.

Every year, he embarked on this little ceremony at the center of some mystical stage. The family watched from inside the house, chuckling and shaking their heads as they glanced out the big window in the kitchen. They drank hot cocoa and ate freshly-baked cookies while he huffed and puffed and looked at the assembly instructions as if they were the Dead Sea Scrolls and he hadn't recently brushed up on his Aramaic.

Those who drove by either smiled or swore, depending on their politics and religious convictions.

Not lost on Mark was the idea that God smiled down from above, while somewhere below, the Devil shook his fist, gazing up at a man he would never have the pleasure of meeting.

It was either heartwarming or deranged, or perhaps a bit of both, as are most things in this world. Especially around the holidays.

One year, perhaps because I had accidentally contracted some of Mark's holiday fervor, or perhaps just because when you are a 21-year-old college student spending day after day in a dry household where there are no R-rated movies to watch and no violent video games to play, there simply isn't much to do, I came up with a crazy idea. I would help.

I marched outside and proudly announced my benevolence to Mark. "I'm here to help," I said.

I'm still not sure if Mark actually heard me, because he just smiled, nodded, and handed me a massive ball of tangled Christmas lights.

We worked together that year, trampling the grass into a muddy quagmire as we trod back and forth, round and round, making sure everything was just right.

We didn't talk much. The only sounds were the periodic, puzzled "huh?" noises we made while trying to figure out the lights and various plastic pieces, the sniffling of our noses in the cold, and the occasional zooming of cars passing by.

It didn't even matter when we were almost finished and suddenly remembered that there was no baby Jesus. The infant Deity had been abducted a year earlier, we recalled, probably by some teenagers who have long since settled into domestic banality today.

It was a fine nativity scene nonetheless, we decided. And Jesus' presence was pretty strongly implied, even if he was nowhere to be seen.

After all, Mark commented as we stood side by side and admired our work, "He is the reason for the entire thing."

HUNTING FOR THE DEAD

My dad loves genealogy. While the term has an academic ring to it, when I was a kid it just seemed like he really enjoyed stalking dead people.

He traced our lineage back hundreds of years, tracking relatives across the globe. At one point, he discovered we were related to Charlemagne. At the time I pointed out that we were technically related to gorillas too, if you went back far enough. At a certain point the dilution of genes renders such claims slightly less impressive to me.

He spent hours upon hours gazing affectionately at family trees and birth records, a distant, happy look in his eyes.

The Internet hadn't yet annihilated the need to physically visit some places to gather information. As a result, my dad traveled to various libraries and town halls where birth, death and marriage records are kept.

He always seemed like a slightly off-kilter version of Indiana Jones. This was partially because he was always poking around in the basements of musty buildings, looking for very old things. It was also because his hair had started to thin and he was going through a period during which he liked to wear hats that, while commonplace in nineteenth century London, seemed anachronistic in modern day America.

The only real difference between him and Harrison Ford was that instead of searching for Nazi gold or the Holy

Grail, my dad was always trying to figure out who someone named Elmer had married 500 years ago.

He would often take me on these investigative trips, which were enjoyable due to his proclivity for mischief. He regularly concocted wild tales in order to gain entrance to private archives and exclusive clubs. I remember him making cryptic comments to me just as we were about to enter buildings where he planned to ask for access to private records.

"Just remember I'm an ambassador from Luxemburg, okay?" he would say under his breath as we entered, giving me a reassuring wink. He'd straighten his khaki windbreaker and pull his wool hat down snugly, as if a bald spot, if viewed by the centenarian dozing at the front desk, would ruin our charade.

Because many of our ancestors lived in Switzerland, my father eventually decided he could only continue his research if we went there in person. He took me first when I was very young. My memory of the initial trip is that I, for reasons that fall entirely outside the purview of my current powers of explanation, felt compelled to wear an itchy tweed Sherlock Holmes-style hat the entire time. Apparently the desire to wear silly caps, like baldness and many deadly medical conditions, is sometimes genetic.

Even in Europe, where the populace has a legendarily high tolerance for outfits that fly in the face of both fashion and common sense, I noticed a lot of people pointing and staring at the little boy sweating profusely beneath woolen earflaps during an Alpine summer.

Most of that first dash across the Swiss cantons is a blur to me. I do remember that the alarm clock at our first hotel malfunctioned, failing to ring in the morning and causing us to miss breakfast.

My father was crushed. "I don't understand it," he stuttered. "How can a Swiss clock be such a piece of garbage?"

A brief, emotional inspection of the clock's underside yielded the answer.

"Ah!" he shouted triumphantly from his perch on the edge of the bed. "It's made in China!"

The broken clock's origin had granted Switzerland a reprieve. When my dad reported the discovery to the woman at the front desk, he did so somberly—the way a man might report finding a dead body in his room.

We visited Switzerland again when I was 16, and by then the world was opening up to me in new ways because I was old enough to walk around on my own without getting stolen.

With my dad using an English-Swiss/German dictionary to trick a clerk into letting him go through archaic birth records, I was free to roam Zurich.

Inside the Rainbow Café, I saw a man smoking a Sherlock Holmes-style pipe with a recumbent black Great Dane sleeping beneath his table. I briefly lamented leaving my matching hat at home.

Five more years would pass before I would be legally allowed to drink in America, and I had recently started reading Ernest Hemingway, so the ability to spend time in a bar was exhilarating. The bubbly elixirs there made every edge seem a little less sharp, every comment a little more lucid, and every goal much more attainable.

Our waitress's name was Nadia and I eventually found myself sitting next to her at the bar as the night outside turned from black to gray.

She told me she was 28. I said I was a junior. I stroked the peach fuzz goatee on my chin. "In college," I added, equal parts hopeful and untrue.

"You go to American University?" she asked. "What courses do you study?"

I said philosophy, and on some level, I have always wondered if I selected that major several years later in an effort to be something less of a liar.

With that, we left and walked across the river, for Zurich has two distinct banks—each bustling with its own palpable and distinct energy.

She soon said goodbye and I set out for my hotel.

A week later, on my last night in Zurich, I was at another café when I saw Nadia pass through the door.

She was with a huge, atavistic-looking man with long, thin braids in his hair and a blue shirt three sizes too small. (It would have been three sizes too big on me.) He seemed to know everyone at the bar, and they all greeted him with almost desperate affection.

When Nadia saw me, she came over to the table, said hello, and discreetly handed me a piece of paper with her mailing address and phone number on it.

I got up to follow her when she left, but she shot me an angry glance and wrapped her arms loosely around the man with whom she had arrived. I spent the rest of the night following her and trying to think of something witty that would make her fall deeply in love with me, but my mind was a total blank. In my head, I was the stolidly committed young American—someone like John Cusack in *Say Anything*—but to everyone else, including Nadia, I was just a creepy little stalker too young, awkward and feeble to even be scary.

Eventually, as I followed her into another bar, she pulled me aside with startling strength. "That man is going to kill you if you keep following us," she said, pointing to the mountain in the blue soccer jersey. "Stop acting like a stupid little kid and go home. Write to me if you want."

I suddenly realized home was on the other side of the world.

All my illusions about having grown into a man as I made my way across Zurich dissipated, leaving me the same gawky, acne-riddled teenager I had been seven days earlier. The only difference was that my dad had given me a little spending money and I was in a country with lax laws regarding the consumption of alcohol.

One night a few days later, back home in the United States, I dove into the ocean with some friends. Nadia's address was in my wallet and all that remained the next morning was a splattering of unintelligible blue ink, not unlike the color of her boyfriend's shirt, on a torn scrap of paper.

The teenage girl I was with when I jumped into the water had a Mohawk on her head and a bullring in her nose. She married me ten years later, and readers of my stories know her as the very tolerant wife who puts up with my various hijinks.

Still, throughout my remaining teen years, I frequently fantasized about saving up some money and traveling back to find Nadia. I figured I would start at the Rainbow Café and go from there. Switzerland was a very organized country, so their employee records probably go back for decades, I thought.

Maybe my dad could even give me some pointers about how to obtain private personal information about strangers.

Now I'm in my late 30s and Nadia, wherever she may be, is therefore nearing 50. She is probably a mother or grandmother, or maybe she's still hopping from club to club as her skin loses its luster, her features become more harsh, and her eyes gradually turn from gleeful to despondent as she encroaches on nonexistence.

And the older I get, the more I understand the allure of stalking people who have been dead and buried for centuries, because they can never make you feel small or vulnerable, and they never tell you to go home. But even better, you know they will always be whatever age you want them to be.

MOVIE STAR

On the first day of filming, my character was being chased across a grassy field.

"Cut!" yelled Ben, the director, beckoning me over to him.

As he cradled his pronounced chin betwixt his thumb and forefinger, Ben offered a gentle piece of direction. "Just run normally in this scene," he advised. "You don't have to run so... weird."

I nodded, feigning thoughtful agreement. "Ahhh," I replied. "I see."

But I was secretly perplexed. I hadn't been trying to affect my movement. I was just running. I wasn't even really acting—I was merely trying to get from one side of the field to the other.

We were in middle school, and owning a video camera magically transformed anyone into a director. Being an actor required two things: being able to speak English and get a ride to the director's house.

We had named our film *L'Aventure*, hoping some French would give the action flick a sophisticated air.

Ben sent us to our starting positions. He hoisted the camera onto his shoulder, took aim and yelled. "Action!"

I took off across the field, pulling up short when the word "cut!" reached me yet again.

"No," Ben called out. "Just run like a normal person. You don't have to do all that other stuff with your arms, and your legs, and your face."

This was distressing, in large part due to the fact that our movie was basically just a series of scenes in which my character fled from an assailant. Kids spend much of their free time running, and it had never—until that moment—occurred to me that I had been doing it incorrectly.

That day's shoot spanned from sunrise to sunset. Actors and crew members gathered around, offering words of encouragement and pantomiming what normal running looked like, in case the problem was that I had never seen it before.

"Do the same thing you are doing now, except don't look so goofy," offered one kid with a friendly pat on the back.

Various enthusiastic hypotheses were posited. Was I holding my breath while I jogged, starving my brain of oxygen so it couldn't appropriately direct my extremities? Was I injured? Was one leg shorter than the other? Was I having a stroke?

My shoes were checked to make sure they were on the correct feet.

"He kind of looks like he's drowning," suggested a rotund kid who had stolen his sister's makeup to get us all "camera ready" that morning.

Everyone went home perplexed.

We began day two by filming one of the only scenes that didn't involve running. My character, having been struck on the head by a villain wielding a tree branch, was unconscious. He'd been discovered by a kindly old farmer, played by a freckle-faced child in a wig, who was nursing him back to health.

The scene opened as my character's eyes did. "Where am I?" I muttered to the geriatric farmer.

"Cut!"

I looked up and waited for direction.

"Matt, can you just speak normally? We don't need you to say your lines in that weird voice."

"I think he has something stuck in his throat," suggested an extra.

"Why is he making those silly faces when he speaks?" asked a scowling co-star. "I don't like it."

I wish I could say they were cruel, but a viewing of the tape the following day confirmed their criticism.

"Why am I running like that?" I mused as we watched footage on Ben's parents' TV. "Is that what my voice usually sounds like?"

We spend so many of our early years imagining that we are other people. For the first decade of my life, whenever I performed any act, no matter how boring, my mind's eye envisioned superheroes and athletes. The youthful imagination is so powerful that it allows these personas to give every activity an added sense of adventure.

Then, sitting in your friend's living room, you find out you are a gangly kid whose closest approximation of a run is an inefficient lope that large, predatory land mammals would find particularly enticing. You don't sound anything like Batman when you talk, and you don't look like Bo Jackson when you run.

By the time I landed my next acting role, I was in college. A friend, who I feel obligated to point out went to film school and now teaches other people about movies, asked me to play a character in a short scene he was filming.

"Is there any running?" I asked hesitantly.

"No, yours is a scruffy, unkempt character who just needs to smoke cigarettes, drink whiskey, and say a couple words," he said. "He's a little messed up, so it would help if you could say the dialogue in a, kind of, weird way."

"Sure," I said with relief. "I can do that."

THE CURE FOR
VAST COSMIC NOTHINGNESS

A few years ago, I found myself marching down a muggy street, surrounded by hundreds of stocky men wearing white beards and red berets. In one hand I held a popsicle stick on which a large picture of one of their faces had been glued. In the other, I grasped a sticky, pink, sugary concoction known as a "Papa Doble."

Amongst the throng, a black plaster bull rolled along.

I had convinced my wife that we should attend the annual Hemingway Days festival in Key West. Ernest lived on the miniscule island from 1928 to 1938.

Today, the festival does not really celebrate the author's life. Instead it focuses on his legacy, which is not exactly the same thing.

Despite his very real accomplishments, Hemingway worked tirelessly to cultivate an exaggerated image of uber-masculinity, virility and machismo. This persona spread so rapidly that it often overshadows the male protagonists of his novels, who tend to be broken, sensitive, nuanced individuals.

Biographer Carlos Baker once wrote that as Hemingway aged, he learned there is "plenty to fear, including the vast cosmic nothingness that Goya named *nada*." In response, Hemingway created an image tough enough and

barrel-chested enough to make Goya's vast cosmic nothingness cower in fear.

So for six days each July, Key West devotes its time and
energy to a man who is part real and part invention.

Upon arrival there, I rushed into Sloppy Joe's—a bar
that serves as the Hemingway festival's hub. It was filled by
hundreds of portly, bearded men who had entered or wished
to enter the annual Hemingway look-alike competition.

"It's very political," one forlorn entrant in the contest
whispered to me during an elimination round, accentuating
his words with a nod and knowing wink. "It's all about who
you know."

Somewhat by accident, I ended up a staunch supporter
of a contestant named "Papa Steve." This happened
because, while I was trying to get closer to the stage, a
woman handed to me a cardboard cutout of Papa Steve's
face, which was glued to a handle that looked like the stick
from the largest popsicle ever frozen.

Not wanting to be rude, I grabbed the sign, hoisted it
into the air, and yelled "Vote for Papa Steve!" over the din.
This was a bit of a miscalculation on my part, for I only
managed to endear myself to a small cluster of people, while
completely alienating the hundreds of supporters cheering
for other contestants.

One danger at the competition is that after several Papa
Dobles—a drink that includes white rum with just enough
fruit juice to prevent it from bursting into flames when
exposed to the sun's rays—people start believing everyone

with facial hair is an unquestionable, scholarly expert on the life and works of Ernest Hemingway.

Forget going to graduate school. If you want people to believe what you say about Hemingway, just throw away your razor.

"Do you know how World War II ended?" I heard one look-alike, dressed in a hunting shirt and matching shorts, say to an enthralled crowd. "Papa Hemingway used the shattered stem of a martini glass to fend off 200 Germans, single-handedly liberating Paris, and when the Fuehrer heard about it, he gave up and popped his cyanide pill."

This was not, in the traditional sense of the word, true. Hemingway was in Paris when it was liberated, but he was there as a journalist, and he was firmly embedded at the Ritz Carlton's bar when the tanks came rolling in. He did have a large stockpile of munitions in his room.

"I think that man who just told us about the martini glass was Hemingway's son," one confused tourist said to his girlfriend as they wobbled away. "He looked just like him."

Wherever we went, the outlandish stories continued. On a chartered fishing boat, in the many shops, and of course in the pubs. And as it turns out, Sloppy Joe's, which mints a fortune each year based on its affiliation with Hemingway, has only a tenuous connection to the writer, because it is no longer located where it was when Hemingway used to spend time there.

At first, all the historical inaccuracies bothered me. "How dare these people play so loose with the facts?" I asked myself.

But I soon realized everyone was simply carrying on with the work Hemingway himself started. They were merely adding a few more layers to his legacy; a few more pounds of muscle, a few more chest hairs, and a few more chapters to his story. A series of new paragraphs in a biography so interesting that death itself had failed to end it.

And throughout the rest of the trip, you could find me telling tourists the types of ridiculous fables that would have made Papa Hemingway proud.

"See this pool?" I said to a woman from Denmark while touring the writer's former home. "He dug it with nothing but a garden spade and the occasional help of one of his six-toed cats. Later that night he wrote most of *For Whom the Bell Tolls.*" I added a nod and a wink: "If you go to the look-alike competition, you should be aware that it's very political."

I had the beginning of a beard emerging, and the woman's breath smelled of Papa Dobles, so she took me quite seriously. I even heard her repeating the tale to a small group of friends as I strolled away.

A friend and I later took part in the annual "running of the bulls." Contrary to its name, this event is actually a lackadaisical saunter of the old and the slightly overweight. A few bovine mannequins on wheels are thrown in for good measure. It's silly, but it's done with genuine love for a story that continues to unfold.

The streets were filled with men in white or khaki, each sporting a vivid red beret as a vague tribute to Hemingway's time in Paris. Their general state of health and age—several were actually forced to use motorized carts to keep up with the group, which was hardly exceeding an amble—belied the famous writer's legendary physical prowess and his brief life. But it didn't really matter anymore.

After all, Hemingway was most famous for one thing: his ability to tell a tale as tall as it was wide. At Hemingway Days, the story is so big, so full of power, that it makes Goya's *nada* a lot less daunting for the rest of us.

FIXING THINGS

Whenever I'm at home and a pipe bursts or a circuit breaker blows, I like to tell my wife that I know how to fix it.

I make this remark while searching for a plumber or electrician in any of the 579 phonebooks someone places on our front porch every week, because I'm not going to put my knowledge—which currently lives in my brain where there are no sharp edges and the risk of electrocution is minimal—to the test out here in the real world.

Most of my understanding of household repairs stems from a three-year stint working at a hardware store in Florida.

I was in college and had already tried out a few other jobs. Finding the market for someone with my unique abilities—which included being able to drink beer while being held upside down and sleeping through alarm clocks so sonorous they caused small earthquakes—a daunting place, I ended up in the hardware business.

I was employed briefly by a different hardware store, but its operators were forced, either by economic constraints or skewed depth perception, to arrange all aisles roughly six inches apart. This arrangement was ideal for waifs and ninjas, but most of us living in the third dimension found it difficult to maneuver through the store.

While working there I heard only two things: shattering goods that followed me as I sidled down the aisles and, not too long after that, the manager firing me.

Eventually I found myself working at a new hardware store with aisles designed for full-sized adult humans.

On my first day I met Don. Don had 11 teeth, a highly unfavorable (some might even say insensitive) view of minorities, and a car valued at $7, which he was "only 13 payments away from owning." The vehicle was in such bad shape that if I drew a picture of it on a napkin, the artwork would be more valuable than the actual Hyundai.

I didn't see much of Don after one of the cashiers got on the loudspeaker one day and announced: "Don, come to the front. There are some police officers here to see you. Don to the front."

I never learned why Don was hauled off to jail, but some people believe it was for something pretty awful. They believe this because it's what I told them, but that is perhaps another story for another day.

Then there was Melody. Melody was 60 years old, carrying on her frame one pound for every year of her life. Come to think of it, she would have had very little trouble getting around in the first hardware store where I worked.

She kept her slight figure by subsisting almost exclusively on vodka, which she mixed with a single molecule of Diet Coke and drank out of a giant travel mug, and carrot sticks she brought to work each day in a plastic bag she had been reusing for years.

Then there was Miss Joan, a woman of indeterminate age except for the fact that she remembered firsthand ducking for cover when Sir Francis Drake shot cannonballs at her shoreline neighborhood in 1586. She spent all her time hunting down cold beverages that had been momentarily set down by employees. Miss Joan would snatch up the plastic iced tea bottles and shuffle off to throw them into the nearest trashcan.

"Shouldn't of left it layin' around," she snapped whenever confronted by parched workers. Her reasons for doing this were never clear, although she frequently liked to point out that unsavory customers would steal anything that wasn't nailed down.

Marco, another employee, had absolutely no money and many, many young children who all seemed to be approximately one year old. I once suggested that perhaps there was a correlation between the two, but he said this wasn't the case.

"It's their mother's, Dog," he said, placing a comforting hand on my shoulder.

Not one to argue semantics, I nodded and asked how many children he actually had.

"Tons," he responded heartily.

He later went on to tell me much of his life story. Marco had joined the Army at a young age, and had traveled to the Middle East, where, he was shocked to learn, people wore different clothes and ate different food than they do in Florida.

In between long periods spent observing other workers so I could belittle them in writing a decade later, I was sometimes coerced into helping customers.

Most of our products were marketed toward people who wanted to kill rodents, weeds or their next-door neighbors.

Popular items included but were not limited to: chainsaws attached to retractable nine-foot poles, a variety of poisons for use in gardens and on children's playgrounds, a flamethrower that was supposed to be used to melt sidewalk ice (in Florida), and large nuclear bombs sold as "turkey deep fryers." These fryers ran on propane and were guaranteed by the manufacturer to spew hot oil and poultry fat in every direction if used on any day the wind wasn't coming from the southeast at exactly four miles per hour.

There were also pool chemicals one needed to wear a Hazmat suit to carry to the front counter. And perhaps best of all, a wide assortment of PVC plumbing fixtures carefully designed so that no three pieces could ever fit together without placing 74 connectors of varying sizes and shapes between them. It was not uncommon for someone to drive to the store to get a single adaptor, only to leave with a PVC creation that looked exactly like a horse's intestinal tract in both length and shape.

In theory, I knew how to fix every customer's problems, and I always explained the solutions to them in the most simple, condescending way I knew how.

"It's really easy (*sigh*)," I would say. "You just need to slice a small hole in your bathroom wall, cut out a section of pipe with a hacksaw, then solder a new one in and toss up a sheet of drywall. Oh, and you might also have to pick up your bathtub and carry it up and down the stairs several times."

I could never understand why customers always returned a few hours later, soaking wet, sporting a large bandage or cast and generally in a bad mood.

Now that I'm a little older, however, I realize that putting any common-sense plan into action can be more difficult than it seems—especially when you are the one doing the actual work. That's why I pay plumbers and electricians rather than doing household repairs myself.

It's also the same reason I'm never disappointed when candidates for elected office don't fulfill every campaign promise right away once they get elected.

Everyone knows how to run a village, county or state: You just spend money on important things and don't waste it on nonsense. But knowing what to spend money on is tricky when public opinion varies vastly and resources are limited.

I've spent most of my adult life working for community newspapers. During that time, I've operated closely with an array of politicians at the local, county and state levels. The thing that usually strikes me when I meet them is that they don't seem much smarter than me, and I'm fairly confident I don't possess what it takes to govern other people.

Some of the politicians I cover hardly seem any smarter than people like Marco and Don—people who clearly didn't even possess the wherewithal to govern their own lives.

There are exceptions, of course, but I find it all a little comforting. Perhaps all of our societal troubles aren't the result of corruption and malice. Perhaps problems are just really difficult to fix, even when you know how.

THE GOOD OLDE DAYS

The parenting books didn't say anything about orcs.

I was pretty sure my daughter would start crying when he came loping toward us, his back hunched, his low-hanging hand clutching an axe, his face twisted into a grotesque, fang-studded grin.

I've certainly seen her cry because of less. So I was sure the ogre's appearance would coincide with our very quick, very premature departure from the Renaissance Fair.

"That orc," I said, utilizing a phrase I had not expected would ever enter my parenting lexicon, "doesn't mean you any harm."

But here's the great thing about small children. They are entirely unpredictable. This 20-pound girl, strapped to my chest and facing outward, looked at the swarthy goblin, gave a playful kick, and grinned.

The bearded men in kilts, their metal mugs clattering as they munched on turkey legs and strode toward the Pickled Gizzard pub. The maidens, their corsets cinched and their hair festooned with ribbons and flowers as they chatted in the King's English and occasionally whipped out their cell phones to check Facebook. My little girl smiled at them all.

While some people go to these fairs to flaunt their leather garb, I go for the anachronisms. For the man in a felt cowl who told us to "park right behind that Pontiac over there" when we arrived in the parking lot. For the guy, dressed as Bilbo Baggins, using a digital camera to snap a photo. For the fortuneteller who told a man that elven blood ran through his veins, then calmly sipped a canned energy drink. And for the industrial jars of Vlasic pickles stacked on the grass just outside the Thunder Pickle vendor's tent.

This was not, I suspect, a strictly accurate representation of life in Renaissance Europe. There were not enough people dying of disease and starvation. Most of these folks could read. Everyone smelled too good. They were pretty short on rats.

Many of the costumes were medieval, and some were Celtic and from the 19th century. There were also people from Middle Earth, which—being a fictional place and time that does not actually exist—doesn't often pop up in historical accounts of the Renaissance.

No, this was not what a typical Renaissance gathering must have looked like. This was, however, exactly what a gathering of 21st-century eccentrics looks like. In that way it was wholly accurate.

"Do you think," mused one of my friends while nodding (very subtly, as one does when making fun of a man with a battle axe) toward a giant fellow with imposing mutton chops, "that it's hard for that guy to stay in character?"

"No," I said. "I think it's probably quite easy. Maybe shopping at Wal-Mart is difficult for him, but not this."

The highlight of the day, at least for me, was watching a fur-wrapped man with a long, heavy claymore sword on his hip as he struggled to enter a portable bathroom. Using these blue plastic boxes is never a task that lends itself to dignity, regardless of attire. But adding a little dance—in which you turn yourself in circles and your weapon prevents entry by clanking repeatedly against the bathroom's door-frame—is a mesmerizing style of performance art on par with fire juggling and belly dancing. (Both of which were taking place a few yards away.)

It even seemed as if his movements were in time with the gentle strumming of a nearby harp, and the playful tittering of a lute that floated in our direction from some unknown location.

Vexed by the unsolvable riddle before him, the warrior finally removed his sword, carrying it sheepishly into ye olde Porta-Potty with him. If he let the weapon's edge touch anything in there, I thought, it would be the functional equivalent of jungle-dwelling hunters who coat the tips of their spears and arrows with poison before going on a hunt.

Away from the bathrooms, people sang and danced in the sun. Their jewelry clattered festively, their ale horns were drained and replenished, and they smiled, which is one human thing that transcends era and epoch.

That's probably why my daughter, who was only six months old, warmed up to them faster than I did. I'm an adult and therefore overly and unnecessarily preoccupied with the clothes people are wearing. With how they style their hair and beards.

My daughter knows better. All she saw was that they were wearing smiles, which really is far more important than what kind of pantaloons they might have slipped into that morning.

Even the orc was grinning.

MASKED GUNMEN
AND LITTLE SHOPS

While they slept at night, five masked gunmen stormed through their locked bedroom doors and then taped and tied up my friends and forced them on their knees at gunpoint for more than two hours while their personal items were ransacked and their safes raided," stated the Letter to the Editor.

My wife and I had just landed in San Jose, Costa Rica, and I was browsing through a copy of the local newspaper.

I carried the publication up to our room, where I tumbled into a recumbent position on the bed. The dense, floral night breeze grew lighter, flitting along the city's dented tin roofs and in through our open window, where it skimmed across my legs and ruffled the corners of the paper.

I continued reading the letter: "The brazen thugs even took time to eat and drink from the mini-bars before taking their leave."

I wondered what type of monster would steal from a mini-bar. I imagined being one of the tourists, my knees aching, my wrists raw from the corrosive adhesive on the generic duct tape.

"Please, take anything you want from the suitcases— take my wife's wedding ring," I would beg. "Just don't touch those peanuts or that nip of vodka. I'll never be able to afford it!"

Our hotel, La Posada, didn't have a mini-bar, which provided a modicum of relief. I prefer all my bars to be full-sized—even super-sized if possible.

Still, the letter got me thinking. Where was I, and how dangerous was this place?

My research before traveling there consisted mainly of viewing an episode of a travelogue program on public television. Perhaps I had fallen asleep or gone to let the dog out during the part where they talked about all the masked gunmen running around attacking tourists.

The publication I was reading, *The Tico Times*, is Central America's leading English-language newspaper, and its reporters managed to chronicle everything unsettling about the region. This particular edition's focus was mainly on the collapse of a bridge that, while bad enough by itself, was exacerbated by the fact that a busload of people plunged into the churning, muddy river below when it happened.

I also read a terrifying article about an American ex-patriot who moved to the Rich Coast to work as a folk artist. (I find folk art only slightly less disturbing than bus crashes and armed robberies.)

Everything else in the paper sounded vaguely familiar: proposed zoning changes, the local animal shelter having a fundraiser, a profile of a new business opening up, a story about pumpkins.

But after a few moments, my heart swelled a little in my chest, because I've been on too many boring vacations. Too many trips during which I ended up eating at a string of chain restaurants where the only threat of violence or tragedy was gastronomic in nature.

It was reassuring to know I was in a different place, and I excitedly went to sleep so I could wake up early and amble about the city.

Shortly after the sun emerged, steam began wafting off of the metal roofs, ensconcing the potted plants that adorned them, forming steamy little second-story jungles. Urban cats strolled wearily back from their nightly patrols, stopping intermittently to sprawl out, present themselves fully and cook in the fresh light.

The activity in the streets below was akin to a major festival in Wisconsin, but is was simply everyone going to work on an average day in San Jose.

An old pickup truck—mottled white and tawny with rust—rolled down the street, tinny music blaring from within and a man on a bullhorn advertising fresh produce that a gang of young boys sold off the vehicle's bed.

Little cars and mopeds were all taking part in some exhilarating race in which no two people were allowed to travel in the same direction at the same time. Stop signs were mere suggestions and lane indicators were laughed off as the unrealistic fantasy of some idealistic planner sitting in an office somewhere far away.

Horn blasts grew to create a symphony—their vehemence, duration and number of repetitions indicating whether they were encouraging other motorists to stop or proceed, speed up or slow down.

Nowhere was off limits, and bicyclists regularly shared the sidewalk with cars and people.

Unleashed dogs of indeterminable heritage accompanied everyone who walked to the stores. The mutts would make quick terrestrial surveys of patches of grass and lampposts whenever their humans ducked into shops. The dogs would soon flop down on a tile stoop somewhere to await their owners' return.

I wandered around, looking for a place to sit and watch the carnival of activity, preferably from behind a solid barrier. But in the absence of rigid American urban planning and with no real understanding of Spanish, it was difficult for me to differentiate between various types of businesses. It was also difficult to tell the difference between stores and homes.

I strolled into what I thought was an abandoned warehouse or prison, only to realize with a grin that I was standing at the entrance to an elementary school.

I thought I spotted a sign advertising chicken, which naturally lured me in, but I found myself the object of several jocular Spanish comments in a stall where a group of mechanics were butchering engines rather than birds. The butcher was in the same building, they indicated, but he was in the next car bay down the street.

Heading the other way, I trundled down a hill and back past our hotel, and entered something common in many countries but almost completely extinct in North America: the tiny store that sells everything.

In the United States, we have big box stores that sell everything, but for some reason they require the square footage of a football field in which to do it. In many other countries, including Costa Rica, people run shops that fit the same amount of merchandise into buildings the size of a single American parking stall.

It is the modern equivalent of the old western general store, but instead of sacks of flour and tonics, they sell Barbie dolls by weight out of a bin and peddle the types of colorful toothbrushes dentists give out for free.

I stepped up into the gooey heat emanating from a café next door.

I had just picked up some basic supplies at the everything shop, employing a technique I use whenever I travel abroad: I walk up to the counter, setting the items I desire upon its surface. No matter what foreign land I'm in, the clerk always says something that sounds vaguely like "Nonsense?" In response I nod calmly, emptying the entire contents of my wallet into a pile and trusting the cashier to extract only a small additional fee in return for my complete trust.

Because the Costa Rican dollar, which is called a *colon*, is fairly feeble, I usually carried several zillion bills in my pocket just in case I wanted to purchase a sandwich or a bottle of beer.

At the café I took a seat on an outdoor patio. It was surrounded by metal bars festively adorned at their apex with barbed wire. If they served "chili with meat," "coffee with milk," or needed me to instruct someone to "close the window!" this would be an ideal place to practice my somewhat limited Spanish lexicon.

"*Café au lait?*" I said with excitement when an elegant young Tica came to take my order.

"*Que?*" she replied with a smile.

I smiled and repeated my order, dumping my money on the small, round table in front of me. Just for fun, I tried a different order:

"*Chili con carne?*"

The woman, who like every person I met in Costa Rica was almost unpleasantly attractive, looked around, probably wondering if I was on the wrong side of the savage security fence.

I smiled a toothy, sweaty grin, unintentionally doing my best impersonation of a serial killer in a horror movie, and we remained at a linguistic impasse for a few moments.

Luckily for me, they only sold two things at the café: coffee and freshly baked sweet rolls. She brought me the default order, which was one of each.

The milk for the coffee came on the side in a little carafe, so I considered my initial order a success.

The ensuing eight days were among the best of my life, a simple truth to which my wife can attest. On most vacations, I experience the nagging suspicion I should be having more fun, or trying more new things. But not in Costa Rica.

We flew on a tiny plane to the country's western coast, landing in the middle of a banana grove and traveling along rutted, largely unpaved roads to Quepos and Manuel

Antonio, where I immediately turned the color of a boiled lobster.

We stayed at a hotel where miniscule arboreal deer and gregarious, chattering squirrel monkeys would saunter and spring, respectively, through the outdoor dining area. Sloths and I would eye each other with respect as we engaged in the same activities at different altitudes—them in the crotch of various trees and me in a growing indentation in the sand below.

It was incredibly foreign for someone who lives in the neatly, rigidly planned settlements of the American Midwest.

The thing I loved most was how little I understood about most of the people, places and things I encountered. The lack of familiarity forced me to actually examine things in a way I never do in the comfort of my own town.

A couple of years later, back in America, I recognized the same look of befuddled wonder in my five-month-old daughter's eyes. "*Oh, right,*" I thought. "*Everything in the world is new and a little bit confusing to her.*"

Every word's meaning is elusive, forcing her to really listen. Every face is new, prompting her to really look.

"Every place is foreign," I realized. "What a wonderful way to live."

BIG CHEESE

It was a few months after my grandfather died and my grandmother was trying to get used to living alone. A troubling smell started wafting through the house.

Eventually, with pinched nose and dripping eyes, she located the source: a lump of Limburger cheese hidden near the back wall of the refrigerator.

My grandfather died the same year I was born. Not down to the minute or anything eerie, but close enough to make it seem as if he was doing his part to maintain a certain balance on the planet. With the entrance of one Geiger, another packed up his metaphysical belongings and headed out the door.

As a result, rather than growing up with a grandfather, I grew up with a set of stories, repeated over and over by my dad, which in time created a man I knew well but had never met in person.

My grandfather, Leon, worked throughout his life for the Dane County Sheriff's Office in Wisconsin, 1,000 miles from where I grew up. He had been diagnosed with cancer at a young age, before even reaching full adulthood. He went on the live to the age of 60, however, and was one of the longest living survivors of his brand of the disease ever documented.

This allowed him to live long enough to develop the multiple other forms of cancer that eventually killed him, which is what happens to anyone who beats a disease, simply delaying their departure and giving other maladies a fair shake at their organs.

On my father's mantle is a framed black-and-white photograph of his dad. He's escorting a recently captured criminal off the steps of a bulbous, old-fashioned airplane, onto the tarmac and presumably into a bulbous old squad car with a comical siren. In the photo, the man is cuffed and my grandfather, just like the other men with him, is wearing an immaculate suit. His necktie is affixed with a perfectly symmetrical knot, his fedora perched at a slight angle atop his head. I gazed at the photo for hours as a kid, trying to recreate the sounds and smells (cigarette smoke, airplane fuel and bourbon, I figured) that would have accompanied the pulpy scene.

Based on this and other photographic evidence, my grandfather does not appear to have been a large man. He was certainly smaller than me. He wore a crew cut, which I have never sported, but also something that looks like the distant cousin of a sneer, regarding the camera with a look that says "I'm not going to pander to you by opening my eyes abnormally wide," which is something I have always done.

It is perhaps odd, and most likely a tribute to my father's abilities as a storyteller, that I remember this man so fondly, because when evaluated from a distance the relationship between my dad and his progenitor—as I guess it was in those days—was not openly affectionate. My dad grew up on the cusp of the hippy movement. He relished rebellion the way my grandfather apparently cherished rules.

Leon was also a devout Democrat, and one of my dad's favorite tales relates to his politics. One day, my dad, still in grade school, obtained a bumper sticker supporting Republican candidate Richard Nixon for president. He did the same thing I would have done, I believe, when he slapped it discreetly onto the back of his dad's car. He didn't do it because he liked Nixon, only because it would surely cause trouble, which is a wonderful thing to behold from just the right distance.

While this should have been a triumphant prank, things went drastically wrong when my grandfather, out of the blue, did a series of nice, friendly things, even inviting my dad to take a trip to a diner where they did (and still do) make the greatest malts and milkshakes ever created. It was on the way out of the diner that my grandfather finally noticed the sticker.

"Wuh…well, will you look at that?" he observed with a crestfallen visage.

"Why would someone do something like that?" he added before getting down on his knees to begin the arduous task of scraping the sticker off the bumper. The way my dad tells the story, he stood there, paralyzed by fear and guilt, with a pink elixir of cream, sugar and strawberries still smeared on the corners of his mouth.

The fear was related to the fact that he would surely be killed with a standard-issue Dane County Sheriff's Office rifle if his role were discovered.

The guilt was prompted by the fact that he believed he had chipped away a small but irreplaceable piece from the foundation of my grandfather's faith in mankind. This man spent his life protecting people, ensuring that they could live in peace and relative safety, and all he wanted in return was the occasional malted milk and the freedom to drive a car that did not openly endorse a troglodyte for president. My dad worried he had robbed his father of that.

But there was one other thing my grandfather wanted in life: Limburger cheese.

That's why I journeyed to meet Myron Olson, the Master Cheesemaker at the Chalet Cheese Cooperative in Monroe, Wisconsin. It is the only place in the country that produces true Limburger.

While I'm unsure which phenomenon caused the other, he looks exactly like my idea of someone who crafts cheese for a living. He is burly in stature and wears a mustache perpetually curled up at each end—not because of any shaving design, but rather because he smiles constantly when talking about the science of turning milk into cheese.

He wields a special knife that, while it would serve its purpose well as a medieval disemboweler, is actually designed for cutting and serving cheese. It features large prongs on the end, and Olson deftly slices slabs then twists and stabs, cutting out little samples of the food from differing depths.

He does so because Limburger is a washed-rind, surface-ripened cheese. While still in its infancy, the cheese is formed into uniform blocks. Employees then rub each block, vigorously and by hand, on pine boards coated in bacteria recycled from generation to generation of cheese, ensuring that the ensuing flavors are of the same family.

The bacteria on the boards today, swimming laps inside a white liquid, are the descendants of the same strain first used in a tiny building down the road that served as the original co-op, all the way back in 1885.

Once the workers—who despite being generally lean have visible signs of disproportionably strong forearms from constantly imbuing the cheese with bacteria—have finished, the little creatures gradually eat their way to the center of each brick, transforming the texture and flavor as they go. It takes about two and a half months for the bacteria's journey to the center of the cheese to be completed.

Olson illustrated this to me by performing an efficient vivisection on blocks of differing ages.

The Limburger is always changing, Olson liked to point out. "Cheese is a living thing," he said.

Limburger is known primarily—almost exclusively—for its odor, which Olson admits is pretty horrible. But once people get past the smell, they enjoy a unique experience. My wife likes to say falling in love with me was similar in some aspects.

Consuming Limburger is like eating butter infused with the flavors of the earth in autumn, in a barnyard, and it is traditionally served up in thick slabs topped with raw onion and mustard, wedged rustically between two pieces of rye or pumpernickel bread, in little rural Wisconsin towns such as Monroe and New Glarus.

These places are the types of communities where someone sporting *lederhosen,* those traditional Germanic leather shorts, doesn't even draw looks of surprise on the street. Limburger is also making a comeback in artisan cheese shops closer to the state capital, where people spend copious time perpetuating images of sophistication. Similar cheeses are even popping up elsewhere, with different names meant to distance the pungent delicacy from its odiferous stigma.

"You hear horror stories about the stink, and unfortunately they are true," Olson admitted. "You almost need a mentor to show you what Limburger is all about."

By leaving a chunk of the stuff in the back of the refrigerator when he left, I suppose my grandfather, whom I never had the opportunity to meet, helped initiate me.

And I should point out, lest anyone get the wrong impression, that shortly before my grandfather died, he went to visit my dad on the farm where he and my mother were working. My grandfather had left behind the agricultural world of his parents for one in law enforcement—one closer to civilization and far more financially secure for his family. He did this only to see his son become a farmer, which I always guessed must have seemed like a backward move, away from the capital and back into the country.

When it was clear his remaining time was growing short —my grandmother even put up a painting of Jesus knocking on the door, as if coming to pick up my grandfather for a road trip—Leon headed out to stay with my mom and dad for a while.

In the most recent picture of him I've ever seen, he is perched atop a tractor, wearing overalls and a real smile rather than a sneer, as he helps plow a field.

I like to think the smile simply could not be pushed aside on that one occasion, perhaps because he was thinking fondly of a piece of cheese, tucked away in the back of the refrigerator, as it ripened to just the right age.

THE TIME MY SISTER JOINED THE CIRCUS

My little sister used to be a circus performer. In my more petty fraternal moments, I tell people it was because she had a second head growing out of her knee, but really her knees are normal.

She was actually in the circus because of where we grew up. And because she is very small.

We lived on a farm. In the summer a circus would roll into town and use one of the fields behind our house to set up candy-striped tents and put on a show. Elephants would lumber around in the pasture where cows usually grazed, and the families that worked in the circus would prepare for the evening's show, either by practicing their routines or by drinking heavily. Sometimes both.

I wanted so badly to join their world, but I never found the opportunity I was looking for. (It would have involved the pretty 30-year-old Bolivian trapeze artist asking me—a 12-year-old kid wearing a rat tail, Reebok Pumps, Skidz pants and a baseball jersey—to run away with her.) Unfortunately, the closest I came was overhearing her telling someone else that getting hair wet makes it stronger, which explained how she was able to tie it to a trapeze and swing violently during her routine without scalping herself.

My sister, on the other hand, became fast friends with the family who ran the elephant portion of the show. I was suspicious of their motives from the start.

Were they trying to make sure the circus had at least one performer from each continent? (My sister was born in Korea, and they seemed to already have someone from everywhere else.) Were they looking for someone tiny for a hilarious caper they were planning? Was this all part of some elaborate and successful plan to make me jealous? Could she possibly put in a good word about me to the trapeze artist?

In any case, my sister ended up traveling to Maine with the circus, where she "performed" under the tent. At the time, I accurately pointed out to my parents that simply posing in a leotard while an elephant picks you up with her trunk and sets you on her back is not really performing. After all, the elephant is doing the work. Despite the logical soundness of my argument, everyone seemed impressed by her ability to smile while being moved around by a pachyderm's proboscis.

Even I had to admit it was glorious. Everything in the show was rickety or rusty—from the moth-eaten safety net below the tightrope to the apparent moral character of some of the performers.

It was everything that is clichéd and politically incorrect about circuses. It exuded an air of danger and unseemliness. It was seedy and it smelled musky—like sugar, wild animals, tobacco, and the perspiration of someone who drinks a lot of whiskey. I loved it.

When dealing with stress in the present, it is inevitably to that memory I flee in my mind. Something about festivity amid detritus comforts me.

When I was a kid, I judged whether I liked a place or activity according to a simple formula: I would ask, "Would my teachers at school take me here on a fieldtrip?"

If the answer was no, I knew I was a fan. If the answer was yes, I decided I would reconsider my verdict 20 years later when I was more easily amused.

The circus passed my test with flying colors.

They even paid me $20 one night to help them take down the tents and put away all the heavy, sharp equipment. Keep in mind I was a random kid who just happened to be lingering on the outskirts of the grounds, hoping to bump into one of the performers as she dried her hair.

A few years later, during my senior year in high school, my class went to an amusement park that looked like it had been made using spare parts gathered from other con-demned amusement parks. The point of going on roller coasters is to be scared, of course, and the efficacy of these rides was breathtaking. Literally.

Then came a decade of prosperity and wealth in America and shoddy forms of recreation seemed to gradual-ly disappear. The only thing left to do was walk around in all the parking lots of sparkling new shopping malls that seemed to be popping up everywhere. For kicks, you could dejectedly wave the little blaze-orange flag provided to you whenever you wanted to cross traffic. The end result, of course, was that everyone spent more money than they had, with some families racking up the type of debt small, struggling countries achieve when governed by a megaloma-niacal dictator.

I got a job at a zoo and ended up working with someone who had previously traveled with the circus. I also worked with a bull camel named Taz, who had performed under yet another big top. During his time traveling with the show, Taz had picked up a habit of smoking menthol cigarettes.

Everyone called my human coworker Guinness, because he was vaguely Irish and they weren't very creative. He, too, harbored love for everything rusty and unsafe, which gave us something in common.

We would sit together at lunch and unleash our harangues between mouthfuls of peanut butter and jelly sandwiches. Nothing was smoky anymore, and it seemed like you were required to wear a helmet and sign a waiver to participate in just about any activity. I certainly don't think most parents these days would let their daughters perform in the circus with a bunch of elephants, I pointed out to enthused nods of concurrence.

True, the less rusty carnival rides we go on and the less vices we partake in, the longer we will live. The problem is, our long lives will be exceptionally boring, Guinness and I reasoned.

I went to the Circus World Museum recently. As I strolled through one of the display areas, I came across what looked like an ancient clown costume. It was the type of clothing that was made before people figured out how to make any garments cheaply, it seemed.

The red and white silk was worn almost to the point of translucence, and through its musty odor, I caught the aroma of something else. It smelled of sugar, wild animals, tobacco, and the perspiration of someone who drinks a lot of whiskey. That alone was worth the price of admission.

CARJACKED

C owering in a basement, watching as the house above me groaned, popped and tried to mutate into rubble, I was having trouble putting my bachelor's degree in philosophy to use.

I was fresh out of college. Unsure where to go or what to do, I quit my job writing at a daily newspaper in Florida and moved back to Massachusetts, where an old acquaintance hired me.

He ran a clandestine remodeling company. Somewhat impressively, he had stayed in business for several months without having any actual experience or training in the field of home improvement. This had the added bonus of making my complete lack of experience seem relatively inconsequential.

I only worked on one house. It was a large, whiteish colonial New England home that was on the Register of Historic Places. I asked my boss if this meant we shouldn't be remodeling the place without a permit.

"Probably," he mumbled while winding up to hit a wall with a sledgehammer.

I painted the exterior three distinct shades of white, because my boss insisted on purchasing paints from the stack of marked-down cans that had previously been mixed into unsatisfactory hues. While they were cheap, one can rarely matched another.

One of my co-workers, a burly man, was later arrested and charged with lewd conduct after allegedly driving around town with no pants on. Due to his unkempt appearance, the police and the local media dubbed him the "Shabby Flasher" while authorities searched for the culprit.

Other co-workers, who came and went irregularly, told me all about the owner of the old white house. They spoke in a hushed, excited whisper, their tongues dripping with saliva as they chewed on the meat of the story. Her name was Kendra, and she had, until a few years ago, been Ken. She was ghostly pale, they reported, and revoltingly ugly. She was, to quote someone who was painting over a piece of duct tape securing a large piece of drywall, "a weirdo."

My boss had a different take on Kendra. "She's really nice," he said. "She pays us on time."

For about a week, I thought everyone was messing with me—playing a trick on the guy who had been away from town for too long. But the household items around which we worked made me wonder. Old mail, photographs and more indicated there was some truth to the stories.

Despite the workers' jokes, I could hear a faint smattering of envy when they talked about her. Kendra was really the closest thing to a superhero any of us had ever encountered in real life. Who else is basically two people? She was like Bruce Wayne, only instead of putting on a bat suit, she put on an evening gown.

One morning, my boss told me we were going to "jack up the house and stabilize the base." I had kept my mouth shut until this point, but his proposal seemed unnecessarily dangerous even by our shoddy standards.

"Isn't that the kind of thing that should be done by a professional—lifting up a three-story colonial building?" I asked.

My consternation only grew when my boss said we needed to go pick up some car jacks.

"Don't they make special jacks specifically for houses? I mean, doesn't a house weigh more than a car?" I said, trying to sound more curious than terrified.

He looked at me the way a physicist looks at a basset hound that just walked into a screen door, speaking slowly and clearly: "That's why we're going to use *several* car jacks."

A few hours later, we had somehow managed to raise the house, or at least the ceiling of the tiny, unfinished basement, by nearly a foot. Under every support beam was a different car jack with a pole or pipe or piece of wood or lunchbox wedged between it and the ceiling.

It occurred to me that if one of the jacks slipped or failed, all the others might decide to follow.

The possibility was finally dawning on my boss. He looked around, seemingly realizing the danger we were in. I had been doing the same thing, but gradually, over the course of several hours, so it was less of a shock. The strain of doing it all at once was too much, especially when we heard a pop and saw the dominos begin to fall.

Just as the first jack failed, a thought popped into my mind. "*My boss is an idiot,*" I said to myself.

In retrospect, there would have been plenty of time to run out of the basement and up the stairs. But we took our imminent death for granted, assuming it was only a matter of seconds. As the roof over our heads started to come down, we simply put our arms around one another and winced in unison for what seemed like hours. But of course, the house was content to settle back into its previous location, scaring us but not physically harming us in any way. As we let go of each other and opened our eyes, the house made a low, contented moaning sound like an elderly person getting comfortable in a chair.

I knew it could have killed us if it wanted to. The house had made its point.

As I shakily made my way up the stairs, I began to question whether I was really cut out for the construction business.

Of course, I had to stick around long enough to meet Kendra. This happened a few days later when we went upstairs to ask what three or four shades of color she wanted the kitchen painted.

Her physical appearance wasn't nearly as shocking as my co-workers had made it sound. Her pock-marked face told of a painful adolescent stint. She seemed to have a real aversion to sunlight, and was therefore a little pale. I couldn't help wondering if it wasn't the sun she was afraid of, but rather all the callous people walking around underneath it all day, just waiting to point and laugh.

As she talked about paint, I craned my neck around to peer into her bedroom. The most striking things about it were the enormous stacks of newspapers. While she had gladly bid farewell to her gender, we suspected she was reluctant to throw away the *Daily News.*

The newspapers gave me an idea. "Perhaps I should return to a career in journalism," I said silently to myself while standing in the old, tri-colored colonial house. "Then I'll get to tell stories like this for a living."

So I did.

ELECTION SEASON

I am mystified by the people who stand outside polling places on Election Day, waving political signs.

Who are they trying to woo? I can't imagine reading newspapers, watching debates and carefully mulling issues like education and the economy, then casting my ballot according to a name on a piece of poster board.

"Well, one candidate agrees with my views on gun control," I would think. "But a stranger has written that other candidate's name in magic marker. I guess I'll vote for him."

Those who think a name scrawled in large purple letters constitutes a compelling political argument, God bless them, perhaps should not be voting at all.

There is little dignity in politics to begin with, but it doesn't help when you try to win elections by employing a tactic most commonly used by people selling $5 pizzas or publicizing "going out of business" sales at discount mattress stores.

I suspect these sign wielders are simply people who really like standing on street corners, but fear our community's draconian loitering laws.

In my opinion, this is one step removed from just walking up to prospective voters, punching them in the face and shouting the name of your candidate over and over.

On the plus side, it is a far more dignified way to engage in politics than watching cable news.

I'm equally befuddled by bumper stickers that state: "Democracy is not a spectator sport."

Of course it's not. It's not a sport at all. It's a form of government that allows citizens to vote (or not vote) according to their conscience. Voting is a civic right—not a civic duty. The law is pretty clear on this. While citizens may exercise their civil rights—free speech, the right to an attorney and the like—they are not compelled to do so.

It's my right to skydive or ask them to make my food "extra hot" at a Korean restaurant, but if I feel those decisions will be detrimental to my well-being, I have the right to NOT do them.

Plus, no one wants everyone to vote. They just want people who agree with them to vote.

While the passing of Election Day brings with it a sigh of relief, it also means bracing myself for the bitterness of those whose candidates lost. I never hear people say: "Well, my candidate didn't win because the majority of voters agree with the other guy's positions."

It's always more backhanded. People didn't vote for your candidate because they were confused, tricked or bullied. Or because they are dumb.

This is the technique of the jilted lover, trying to explain the reason a woman has chosen someone else over him. "She loves him and not me," he says. "She must be blind."

I wish people would be more honest, rather than trying to couch their disappointment in faux wit.

"I think people who don't agree with me are dumb," should be the bumper sticker.

The truth is, people tend to vote according to their upbringing and life experience. So what you are really saying is, "I don't like people whose lives are different from my own."

What I quite enjoy is seeing just how narrow the gap is between "this person doesn't agree with me about public transportation" and "this person is the spawn of Satan."

Also, my voting friends clearly believe that, like jogging, it doesn't count unless you post something about it on Facebook.

One thing we can all agree on is that no more canvassers is a good thing. For the next several months, I can rest easy knowing any stranger who shows up at my house unannounced is probably only there to rob me or convert me to their religion, both of which are better than trying to win my vote.

What would possess an adult human being to go door to door, begging people to stop cooking dinner and chat about who they plan to vote for? At least the children who rang my doorbell on the night of Halloween entertained me with their ornate costumes. These political campaigners were just wearing regular, boring coats and goofy smiles. Rather than asking for a Snickers, they wanted my vote.

They also seemed unaware that I was holding a crying baby, keeping a howling dog at bay with my foot, listening for the pot on the stove to boil over, and trying to remain polite.

"I see you live in utter chaos," they'd eagerly chirp. "I'd like to stand here and talk to you for 20 or 30 minutes about a highway tax."

"At the very least," they'd continue, "we should stand here awkwardly with the door ajar and let all the heat out of your house."

Sometimes these people do make compelling arguments. But I have one question I like to ask, no matter who they support.

"Does your candidate's name," I say, "look good in purple magic marker?"

MY BABY'S SHRINKING HEAD

I was sure my daughter's head was shrinking.

It began with a casual visit to the doctor's office shortly after she was born. The kind at which people in smocks weigh, measure and poke your child.

Anyone who has tried to obtain the exact measurements of an infant knows the task is roughly as easy as figuring out the precise number of angels who can dance on the head of a needle. Nurses tend to make a loose loop of flexible measuring tape, then attempt to lasso your infant's cranium like someone in a Wild West show roping a bucking calf.

During one visit, the nurse, satisfied that my squirming daughter's head had briefly occupied the space inside the loop, jotted down an arbitrary number and went on with her day.

Three months later, at the next checkup, we saw a different nurse. The kind I doubt cuts many corners in life. She was the type of woman who weighs flour when baking, because air pockets in a measuring cup might lead to tiny, unacceptable irregularities. The kind of person who makes appointments for times like 5:43 p.m.

She measured our daughter with the intense gravitas I usually only show when selecting my annual Thanksgiving turkey.

She insisted on wrapping the tape tightly around little Hadley's head, then cinching it—like an equestrian trying to get a saddle onto a bloated horse—before carefully writing down the measurement. She marked the number with her thumb, then looked at it from several different angles to make sure it was correct.

This all seemed fine until the doctor arrived several minutes later. Looking quizzically at a computer-generated chart that showed our daughter's head shrinking by several inches over the course of three months, she uttered the most terrifying sound a medical professional can make.

"Huh?"

I'm 36 years old, and I still think back with vexation and horror at the time, when I was a kid, that a doctor quietly muttered "Hhmm" while giving me a physical. Three decades later, I sometimes wake up in the middle of the night wondering, "*What was it? What about me was so strange that someone who had read thousands of pages of medical texts was so surprised? What is wrong with me?*"

Hadley's doctor was eventually able to collect herself, and this time I wasn't leaving without an explanation.

"It would appear, if you just look at the chart, that your daughter's head is much smaller than the last time she visited us," she said without any of the horror that should accompany those words spoken in that order.

"I knew something terrible was going to happen," I thought. "The universe couldn't just let me have this one thing. Well, that's just great."

There were two possibilities, as far as I could tell.

The first was that Hadley had the Benjamin Button disease, and she was aging in reverse. But that seemed unlikely, since most of Scott Fitzgerald's writing has little or no connection to the actual world.

The other, far more likely scenario was that someone had placed a curse or hex on my family. People threaten that type of thing all the time, usually after they show up in the court report of the local newspapers I edit. It was only, I mused as I examined my daughter's forehead, a matter of time before something like this happened.

Then I remembered hearing about a condition called microcephaly. But those afflicted with microcephaly simply have small heads. Their heads are tiny from the start. I couldn't remember anything about heads that were actively getting smaller.

After staying silent for long enough that I was able to think all these horrifying thoughts, the doctor smiled and shrugged: "I wouldn't worry about it. Wiggly babies can be hard to measure."

"We'll just keep and eye on it and makes sure her head has grown next time we see her," she added, a little too flippantly for my taste.

"Or what?" I wondered. "Is there treatment if her head is getting smaller, or do I just bring her straight to an early 20th-century carnival sideshow and try to raise money for many small but fashionable hats."

I have long wondered why people whisper when they pray. Is the idea that God has really good hearing, so He can hear you all the way from His heavenly throne without the need to shout? Or is it—and this is the more likely answer—that most people are hoping none of their mortal peers will hear that they are asking a supreme being for thicker hair rather than world peace?

In any case, that's the voice I heard in my head that afternoon, sitting nervously in the doctor's office.

"If her head grows, I will be so thankful," I whispered to myself within the relative privacy of my brain. "So truly appreciative."

It turns out the doctor was correct. An imprecise measurement—or perhaps an overly precise measurement, if you share my view on the matter—was the culprit. After all, the initial measurement, slapdash though it was, didn't cause any consternation until the more rigorous nurse showed up.

Just further proof that most of the world's problems are caused by people who take their jobs far too seriously.

Either way, I could safely rule out black magic.

Today, Hadley has grown into a robust, full-sized toddler with a matching head. In fact, her cranium is practically bursting right now, as the brain encased in it races to ponder every word she hears, every sight she sees and every household item she shatters.

She splits her time between trying to master language and running around our house performing trust falls without warning the rest of us that we are expected to catch her as she plummets off the dinner table.

The early magic of child rearing is often replaced by the physical and mental exercise of keeping her alive and entertained. After all, your child looks slightly less angelic when she kicks you in the face on the way to the urgent care clinic, or when she is flushing your favorite book down the toilet.

But this fall, as Hadley and I head down to the supermarket to select our Thanksgiving turkey, I'll remember the time I briefly thought her head was getting smaller. As I weigh, measure and poke the big bird's carcass, displaying all the assiduity of a very serious nurse, I will take a moment to give thanks for my daughter's growing head.

HARD CIDER

"So it's magic?" I asked hopefully.

I was interviewing a scientist about biofuels and things weren't going well.

He was kind enough to speak to me as if I were a ten-year-old child who had neglected to take my Ritalin as he explained the alchemic process that allows cars to somehow run on corn and other organic material, but still I couldn't wrap my mind around it. Noticing my protruding belly and the way I was freely perspiring in a fifty-degree laboratory, he attempted one last time to use terms I could understand.

"It's very similar to the way alcoholic beverages are made," he began, speaking slowly.

Encouraged by the way my head involuntarily perked up, he continued.

"The sugars in grain or grapes are converted into alcohol in beer or wine—it's the same with corn in ethanol. It's basically whiskey."

He had to yank away a jar of the stuff as I reached for it, but he was correct in guessing that connecting science to booze would arouse my attention. Still, the details eluded me. Adult beverages are like internal combustion engines and good stories—I have no idea how they are made, and I haven't a clue how they work.

In high school, a chemistry teacher told us how to ferment apple cider, but it ended up tasting horrible, causing intense abdominal cramps and containing absolutely no alcohol. Oh, and did I mention it caused the type of diarrhea usually reserved for dysentery? Needless to say, the party we threw to celebrate its completion was an unmitigated disaster.

Later in life, I found myself in possession of something called "Mr. Beer," which not entirely coincidentally was my nickname throughout much of college. It was a home brewing kit, but rather than fresh ingredients, Mr. Beer, which was plastic, by the way, called for a revolting pre-made syrup you had to order online.

"Matt's Honey Ale" might have been delicious. I don't know, because it was also highly explosive. The bottles that did not detonate during the fermentation process were opened only to spurt foam on the ceiling, drapes and into the eyes of the brew master. Drinking something that heavily carbonated, I worried, would be the same as injecting air into my veins.

Then one summer—a year after my failed interview with the scientist—a friend asked if I would be interested in fermenting "some" cider with him. By "some," I learned he meant 55 gallons of freshly pressed apple juice from an orchard in a nearby town. He said it would be simple, and by "simple," I learned he meant labor intensive, confusing and generally difficult.

The same friend, who is a couple years younger than me, close to seven feet tall and went to an Ivy League school that probably wouldn't allow me to clean its toilets, stopped by my house a few years after the cider adventure and was without his trademark beard.

"What happened?" I asked.

"Oh, I shaved it so it would be easier for the doctors to work on me," he replied.

Noticing my puzzled look, he went on. "I had just a little touch of the cancer," he said in a type of nonchalant tone I use when telling my wife they were out of ripe bananas at the grocery store.

He told me he had been diagnosed with thyroid cancer. Apparently, surgeons had to remove the gland, which I later learned from a dictionary regulates the human body's metabolism.

"I'm still a little radioactive from the treatment, but I shouldn't pose any threat to you," he said.

He told me he needed to take synthetic thyroid medicine for the rest of his life, but he is the type of man to be prepared for anything. I wasn't surprised to learn that he also planned to learn how to kill pigs and remove their thyroid glands, because in the event of a near apocalypse that wiped out all the pharmaceutical manufacturers, he wanted to know how to make his own replacement medicine.

But back to the cider.

For starters, transporting 55 gallons of any liquid from the orchard to one's house is a somewhat awkward undertaking. It's like trying to get the water from one swimming pool to a new one 15 miles away, except this water was brown and sticky. And once we got home, I remembered something I had learned about 30 minutes earlier: large containers full of apple juice are extremely heavy, especially when the designated cider-making room is up two flights of stairs.

Yeast, I found out, is the ingredient that turns the sugars in juice into alcohol, so we poured some into the containers. We placed little air locks—devices that allow gas to escape but prevent air from getting in (I reiterate, this is clearly some kind of magic)—on top of the mouths of the kegs and waited. The juice finally started to gurgle, bubble, and—my wife particularly liked this part—make the entire house smell like rotten apples for about a month. It smelled like a dog whose diet consisted exclusively of Apple Jacks had been shitting in our guest bedroom.

Eventually the smell died down and I forgot about the kegs. They sat in my house throughout the winter, and at the dawn of the next summer, my friend informed me it was time to bottle the cider, which would be "simple."

This, I soon discovered, is the most difficult part of the process. There is siphoning involved, and something called "racking" (which doesn't involve any racks at all, I was surprised to learn).

It also involves sterilizing hundreds of bottles. My wife can tell you it is difficult for me to build up the courage to wash a few plates and some silverware. And I regularly catch her rewashing the dishes after I've had a go at them, because apparently I do an unsatisfactory, or as she puts it, "unsanitary" job. Sterilizing hundreds of anything seemed beyond my ability.

Somehow we managed to bottle it all, but to my horror, it tasted terrible. The closest my palate has ever come to tasting this crap was when I ate ten boxes of sour candy on a dare as a kid and gave myself the equivalent of a sunburn on the inside of my mouth.

I later learned it is best to wait and let cider settle and age once in the bottle. So, to my delight, there was more waiting involved.

In the meantime, I decided to learn a little more about the beverage I suddenly owned in profusion. I found an article on George Mason University's website proposing theories why cider, once the most popular alcoholic beverage in America, fell out of favor.

Apparently, from the early 18th century to 1825, even children drank hard cider with breakfast and dinner, which makes me suspect being a schoolteacher back then was even more of challenge than it is today. Yes, these days you have to deal with issues of declining state funding and globalization, but back then, all the children were drunk when they got to class in the morning.

The article also said John Adams drank a tankard of hard cider every morning, which I assume he followed up with an aspirin the size of a soccer ball and a short nap.

The real reason cider fell out of favor, at least according to this paper, was not what I expected (the acrid taste and piercing, immediate headache it induces). Cider was simply replaced by soft drinks, which back then had cocaine in them, which—let's be honest here—is a pretty good selling point.

I don't drink soft drinks, but eventually my homemade cider became palatable. Later, it became delicious.

It also didn't kill me, which it turns out was a risk when I got in the bootlegging business. A nurse later told me that some people accidentally produce methyl alcohol, rather than ethyl alcohol.

"What's the difference?" I asked.

"One gets you drunk," she answered. "The other one kills you."

So now I like cider. I'm even considering drinking a tankard of it every morning, once I figure out what exactly a tankard is (all I know is it sounds large).

Most importantly, however, I finally understand how fermentation works. Next I'm going to figure out how the engine in my car functions. If there is any time left when I'm done with that, I'll get to work figuring out how to write a good story.

PHILOSOPHY

Calling home from college to tell your parents you are switching your major to philosophy and theology is a rather sobering experience for everyone involved.

For them, it is much like a call from jail, only worse because instead of a one-time bail payment, you are essentially informing them you will require financial subsidies for the rest of your life. For you, it is perhaps even more difficult, because there is a slight chance this is the final straw and they will decline to pay for your food for the next fifty years. In my case, I had already made the call from jail a few years earlier, which surely did not help my chances.

The reaction from friends was also less than enthusiastic.

"You know you can't sleep on my couch after you graduate, right?" one said in a matter-of-fact tone.

A more compassionate friend fell silent for a moment, consulted with someone on his end of the line in hushed but insistent tones, then returned: "Well, I'm sure you can live in our garage for a while until you find a job at Wal-Mart or something."

At first I thought they were all kidding. "That's a good one," I would respond with a condescending chuckle. "But things like ethics and truth and God are really interesting. I'm sure someone will pay me to think about them."

A few weeks later, I bumped into a former classmate who had graduated at the top of his class with the same degree a year earlier. He was an intellectual giant who always made me feel stupid in the classroom, but when I ran into him, he was very polite. I said hello, complimented him on his nice blue smock and asked how things were going. He greeted me with a smile and asked if I needed help finding anything, which I believe was part of his job, and added that frozen hamburgers, car batteries and hammocks were all on sale that day.

Oddly enough, the only person who supported my course of study was my editor at a newspaper in the city of St. Augustine, where I worked during college. Yet even she warned me that I "might never get paid for writing about philosophy or God."

I pledged that one day I would, then forgot all about my ambitions and learned about the most interesting personalities imaginable for four (okay, five) years.

And when it comes to compelling personalities, no other assemblage of people even comes close to philosophers and theologians. I don't know if it was the syphilis or the mustache, but Nietzsche was certainly a more colorful character than Brittany Spears will ever be. Setting aside the fact that Nazis twisted and zealously embraced his work (it wasn't the first time they got carried away), he might well have been the most dynamic thinker of the past 1000 years.

All the way back in 400 B.C., the Greek philosopher Diogenes was hanging out in Athens, living in a barrel with a pack of feral dogs and founding a school of ascetic philosophy known as the Cynics, which many people are surprised to learn was not really a very cynical school at all. He was also, according to some sources, fond of barking at passersby and marking whatever served for fire hydrants in those days.

Then, of course, there were the flagellants, a widespread group of Christian monks who whipped themselves regularly. Perhaps unintentionally, they also made countless college students giggle uncontrollably at their chosen name a few hundred years later. "The farters," as we liked to call them, were indeed fascinating.

There was also Blaise Pascal, who lived in France in the 17th century. Pascal claimed that since the existence of God can be neither proved nor disproved, the wisest course of action, or at least the most practical one, is to believe in Him or Her.

The rationale was essentially that if you believe in God and there isn't one, no harm done. You'll never even know you were wrong. On the other hand, if you walk around declaring that there isn't a higher power and turn out to be incorrect, there might be a fairly awkward conversation with someone much bigger and stronger than you after you die. The dialogue would invariably be a short one, starting with you saying something like "Uh, oh..." and ending when you were struck by a lightening bolt, sent on a one-way trip to Hell or reincarnated as a dung beetle.

Perhaps my favorite personality, however, belonged to Jeremy Bentham, an English social philosopher who lived from 1748 to 1832. According to Dagobert Runes (yes, that's a real name) in his 406-page book *Pictorial History of Philosophy*, which incidentally contains a whole lot of text too, Bentham left his entire estate to the University of London. He did so with the provision that his remains be present at all meetings of the university's board. Runes' book includes a picture of Bentham's dead body, sitting atop a chair, its hand resting on a cane. The head atop his shoulders is wax, but the actual head rests between Bentham's feet, shriveled and black, preserved in the tradition of South American headhunters.

STOP AND SMELL
THE MANURE

I once found myself in one of Wisconsin's countless small agricultural hamlets. I overheard a woman nearby, speaking in a crusty East Coast accent and waving her arm violently enough to make her black leather jacket creak. She lived in one of the shiny new subdivisions lurking on the edge of town, she said. "It smells awful in my neighborhood—I hope we can do something to get rid of that farm next door," she continued.

She seemed nice enough, despite having clearly splashed around in an aggressive perfume before heading out that evening. I can only assume she was trying to create an olfactory force field around her body to fend off the smell of cow manure. So I bit firmly into my tongue and didn't mention that the farm had been there for generations and she had lived there a few months.

I had been there a few years by then, and I was already brimming with the zealous pride of a convert. Before I moved to the Midwest, which is by all definitions flyover country but also grows a large portion of the country's food, I heard it was a frigid place brimming with cheese. I was told hefty people of Scandinavian descent puttered around in green and gold, balancing a bratwurst in one hand and a fistful of beer in the other, occasionally stopping when they saw something of interest to exclaim a slightly out of breath "uff da," then waddling along on their amiable ways.

Early on, in a misguided attempt at cultural sensitivity, I often derided people for such descriptions. "That's ridiculous," I would say. "Those are just antiquated stereotypes. I'm sure people there are just like people everywhere else."

Imagine my surprise when I arrived and before leaving the airport waded through a sea of cheese blocks, cheese curds, cheese shaped like a cow, cheese shaped like the State of Wisconsin and beer cheese soup mix. It turned out the picture society had painted of this place for me was in fact far more accurate than I anticipated.

Today, there are within thirty minutes of my house no fewer than ten breweries—one I could hit if I threw a stone out my window. (I wouldn't; that would be like the Cookie Monster torching the tree where the Keebler Elves live.)

During much of the summer, my drive to and from work doubles in time when I find myself blissfully stuck behind off-road farm vehicles that look like they could eat a field of corn and a large military tank for breakfast.

Every other person I meet has a name that ends in "-son," which I assume is a relic pointing toward a shared Scandinavian heritage.

But the best thing about Wisconsin is the Cow Chip Toss. To be more specific, the best thing about Wisconsin is the fact that no one seems to think the Cow Chip Toss is weird.

Shortly after moving there, while writing for a local newspaper, I attended this large festival in Sauk Prairie. There, otherwise normal men, women and children picked up chunks of cow manure and tried to see how far they could heave them. Their form in the "cow chip toss" was immaculate enough to make an Olympic discus competitor's jaw drop.

I later discovered that cow manure was an important part of life for many early settlers in the American Midwest. Not only was it a decidedly inevitable byproduct of livestock, it also provided a free source of fuel to burn on cold winter nights. While no longer used to heat homes, it is remembered fondly each year at the Wisconsin State Cow Chip Throw, which takes place around Labor Day.

In 2006, the Wisconsin State Cow Chip Throw Committee released a set of rules that I still have in my possession. I treasure them, keeping them in the same drawer as the photos from my wedding and the awards a professional newspaper association has accidentally given to me.

Each contestant in the competition is allowed to select two pieces of crisp, sun-hardened manure out of the back of a wagon. The pieces must be at least six inches in diameter and may not be significantly altered to enhance their ergonomic traits. If the manure breaks apart in midair, the portion traveling the furthest is measured to gauge the contestant's official score. Of the two initial throws, only the highest score is kept. Contestants are not permitted to wear gloves, and a common trick used to provide maximum grip is to lick one's fingers before throwing a chip. Men and women compete separately, and the winners are eligible to move on to compete in the World Cow Chip Throw. In 2006, it took place in a place named Beaver, Oklahoma.

It should be noted that one man—Greg Neumaier—once managed to achieve a stranglehold on the Wisconsin Cow Chip Toss for seven years running, between 1991 and 1997. His best distance, achieved in the first year of his streak, was 248 feet, which I feel compelled to note is nearing the length of a football field. A woman named Terry Wallschlaeger held an even more impressive streak, having won the state-level competition 13 years in a row. Her best distance was just over 155 feet.

While outsiders may be tempted to envision a group of backward, inbred hicks participating in the Cow Chip Toss, that's not really the case. There are overalls to be seen. It should be noted that they are not worn ironically, but rather are stained, sun-bleached clothing that farmers were simply too tired to change out of after a long day at work.

The most enthusiastic contestants in the toss are those who take part in the corporate competition, which pits employees from nearby office buildings and restaurants against one another. A common costume on these contestants involves the iconic black-and-white, yin-and-yang pattern made popular by the Holstein cow. While this may seem a little odd, I should point out that beer is ubiquitous at this festival, so things tend to seem strange only in retrospect and after the hangover has temporarily taken leave.

While manure is the centerpiece of the festival, it is surrounded by an array of activities. People attend the event to eat ice cream, watch country and classic rock bands perform, and, as I mentioned, to drink beer by the hundred-weight.

While newspaper and radio are used to some extent in the promotion of the event, a Trojan cow, modeled after the fabled wooden horse that allowed the Greeks to lay siege to the City of Troy, is perhaps the most vital component of the advertising plan. The cow, which weighs approximately 2,600 pounds and was constructed using an angle-iron frame and a primarily wooden outer layer, also features an udder made from—get this—real cowhide. Seventeen hinges ensure that the cow—which travels in parade processions throughout the area, leaving in its wake pieces of cow manure—is functional. The head is moveable and a trap door allows children to sit inside the beast, tossing cow chips out the back as they head along the parade routes.

My first year at the Cow Chip Toss was like a toe being dipped in the water. Rather, it was like a pair of trembling fingers grabbing hold of a piece of manure. It does not come close to representing my complete immersion in Midwestern life, but it did operate like a gateway drug, opening my eyes to a variety of new experiences.

I've eaten something called *lefse*, which is a Norwegian flatbread made from potatoes and old lederhosen.

I've stuck my head out the door in the morning, noted the temperature was 10 degrees Fahrenheit and called back to my wife, "Honey, it's warmer today."

I've attended a cheese festival in Monroe, where I consumed a Limburger and onion sandwich while listening to a yodeling competition and, I'm not sure I even need to point this out anymore, drinking an ale.

Yodeling is often poked fun at, but after listening to it first-hand, I realized it requires remarkable linguistic dexterity. It's as if an auctioneer, midway through emitting a succession of machinegun-fire numbers, suddenly burst into a festive song, prompting everyone to bounce around and spill their lagers.

And yes, even the healthiest of my Wisconsin friends seemed to be carrying around a little extra insulation so that, just in case it gets very cold very quickly, they will be sure to stay warm.

I am not immune to this particular phenomenon, and I think fried cheese curds might have something to do with it.

I know it's politically incorrect to perpetuate stereotypes, but in the Midwest they seem to ring a little true. Yet I eventually noticed a disturbing trend: People, many of whom were transplants from the coast such as me, had developed an urge to stamp out the things that made this region unique.

They wanted to make Wisconsin seem more urbane and more like everywhere else. They wanted to be able to shop at the same stores and restaurants they patronized back in their home states, and they wanted to cut down on the consumption of cheese and beer. They disliked the things I treasure most—like the opportunity to get stuck behind a vehicle with ten-foot wheels that looks like something from *The Road Warrior* but painted bright green or red.

I fear someday soon, these well-intentioned but misguided residents will try to stop people from competitively throwing cow chips—surely they are covered in germs, after all—and Wisconsin will slowly cease being interesting. Eventually, it will become a mind-numbing succession of chain retailers located near highway off-ramps.

In the end, they'll probably get their way—leaving behind as little of the culture they usurped as did many other invaders before them.

As for me, I'll continue enjoying local cheese, and local beer, and picking up local cow droppings and throwing them, because as far as I can tell, I live in a place that is, for the time being at least, like no other.

From time to time on my way home from work, I even roll down the window and take in the lovely smell of cow manure when I'm driving past a farm.

AM I WRONG?

I recently had to go to the doctor for a cancer screening. The circumstances surrounding the event having woven themselves into a baroque tapestry of anxiety and existential dread, I took off my clothes and readied for the worst.

The highlight of the afternoon was probably when I was given a clean bill of health.

But it's possible that the real apex of my day actually came twenty minutes before that, when the woman who was prepping me for the procedure smiled kindly and said, "I hope this isn't weird for you, but I just want to say how much I enjoy reading your stories in the newspaper."

It was weird. It was also wonderful. In fact, I think it was the nicest thing anyone has ever said to me while I was wearing only socks and a very large paper towel.

I forgot why I was there for a moment and basked in the strangeness of my current situation. Scary is bad. Scary and weird, though? That, to me, is infinitely more bearable.

It was a small moment in her day, I'm sure, but it's one that will stay with me for a long time, because she reframed my experience in a way that made it more manageable.

The universe allowed me to leave with my health, and she allowed me to leave with a great new story. It was, in every sense, a good day.

That—the ability to tell stories in our own unique voices—is our species' greatest accomplishment. The power to make the terrible funny, or the funny tragic, or the mundane magical—all through a series of grunts, growls and the occasional adverb. These are the kinds of powers usually reserved for mythological deities.

We tend to call the most powerful of these narratives "scripture." Some have power thought to be so great that the books themselves are treated as magical items.

The thing about religion—the beauty of it, I think—is that it is cloaked in mystery. It can be frustrating, but its opacity and arcane attributes leave infinite room for the narrator. That is why, after thousands of years of religion on Earth, you have so many people telling so many slightly different stories about God. ("Theology" literally means, "words about God.")

Anyone who tells you they, and they alone, hold the key to these mysteries is probably trying to sell you something.

Everyone tells, reads or hears these tales, including Christians, Muslims, Buddhists, Sikhs, Taoists, Atheists (whose adherents, ironically, are sometimes the most preachy), and Agnostics (it may be the most logical position on the matter, but my goodness it is a missed opportunity to feel passionately about something).

The great thing about scripture, and the one thing all world religions have in common in their teachings, is the co-existence of mutually exclusive ideas. The same book will teach love, tolerance, hatred, war, fear, death, immortality, vengeance and forgiveness.

The Christian Bible, for example, says God doesn't want you to wear a poly-cotton-blend shirt, and that you will only further irritate Him if you plant tomatoes and broccoli in the same field. The same book goes on to suggest that both tax collectors and prostitutes are on their way to heaven. In the Bible, God tortures Job, an innocent man of great faith, in what amounts to a mean-spirited prank. The same God later suffers and bleeds, by choice, for the salvation of all of humanity.

While God—or the lack thereof—remains a mystery to us, the way that people give and receive their religious stories can tell us a lot about who they are. Everyone worships one form of God or another. It can be Ganesh, Jesus, Free Speech, the Right to Bear Arms, or the Almighty Dollar.

Someone who likes carnage tends to latch onto those parts of their particular holy book, while those who wish to live in a world of tenderness can recite all those verses by heart.

And because the idea of God is such a vast enigma, we all get to do it. Every single human being on the planet. Even those who believe with absolute certainty that there is no supreme deity can thank this mystery, because it allows them to feel passionate conviction without the need for concrete proof.

God is an idea that is simply too big for one religion, one book, or one political party.

It all revolves around faith, however, and that is the most treasured trait in any audience, regardless of the narrative.

I will say that how people tell a story matters, and so does how they listen. Being right or wrong is not everything. Nor is it the only thing. You can be simultaneously correct and insufferable. You can even be wrong yet kind.

So when you are staking out your vehement position on God, or presidential politics, or some silly little issue before the school or village board, try to be right, of course. But also know that being right, or being wrong, aren't the only things that matter. In the end, at least when it comes to the big questions in life, we never really get to find out who had it right anyway.

But the way you are right or wrong—and the way you choose to worship your personal Gods—says a lot about you. And that remains true regardless of the altar at which you bow down.

LIKE A HURRICANE

I f interpreted literally, "We're baby-proofing our house" actually means: "We're installing security measures to prevent babies from entering our home."

Whenever people tell me they are "baby-proofing," I briefly imagine they called an inspector who came and tested their home. "Ah, I see the problem here," he'd say as his detector started chirping near a basement wall. "You've got babies."

"Remediation is a two-step process. First you'll need to get them all out of here, then you need to seal up the house to keep them from getting back in."

"When you're done, I recommend installing a baby detector so you know right away if they do come back," he'd add as he climbed into his van and drove away.

There is already a baby in our house, and we're pretty sure she's staying. And we are trying to make our home safe enough that she can explore it without being cut, electrocuted or bludgeoned. While doing this, we look a lot like those frantic people you sometimes see on the evening news, boarding up their homes and slinging sandbags over their shoulders as they await the arrival of a violent hurricane.

Our storm will continue growing for the next 18 years. And unlike the people on TV, we cannot, at least not legally, just pack up the car and flee when things get really bad. We are required by law to feed this storm, keep it safe, and at some point, even teach it to operate a motor vehicle.

Like any good hurricane, her goal is simply to achieve maximum chaos.

This isn't how we imagined it. A year ago, we had lazy conversations about easy, theoretical problems that could be fashionably solved. Browsing the Internet and smiling at each other, we spoke in soft voices as we tried to decide which color safety latches would look best on our cabinets.

"Oh, look at those brass ones," my wife said. "Those would really compliment the wooden doors."

At one point before our storm made landfall, we actually had a lengthy—somewhat heated, if I recall—debate about which shape we preferred when selecting the safety covers for our low-lying electrical outlets.

"Those square ones look a little clunky for my taste," I said. "The oval ones are a bit more refined, don't you think?"

I was like the owner of a beach home, wasting precious hours deciding whether I wanted to nail pine or cedar boards over my windows.

"Honey," I might as well have called to my wife over the roar of the approaching typhoon. "Do you think I should use stainless steel nails, or galvanized ones? I think the stainless would look much nicer."

Today, questions of aesthetics have long been usurped. The storm is here, and our focus is squarely on survival.

As our hurricane crawls around, sticking her fingers into some things, smashing others, and struggling so mightily to decipher which items are and are not edible, we try to rearrange our home so it will not kill her.

Piles of books, upside-down chairs, even the dog have been called in to support the cause, being used to build makeshift barriers as we block off one hazard after another.

To further complicate matters, we are actually trying to teach this destructor to walk, which, when I write it out, makes about as much sense as giving a shotgun to a rampaging gorilla.

When our hurricane goes to sleep, my wife and I huddle together in silent relief. Sometimes we even have small social gatherings with other parents.

On occasion, we watch sports. And there is no sadder, more middle-aged sound than a group of adults whispering "Yay!" The hushed cheer, which takes place when a local athletic team scores a run, basket or touchdown after 7 p.m., is usually followed by nervous glances all around. Everyone strains their ears, listening intently to hear if the children have awoken.

This is a new, neutered version of sports fandom.

Yet somehow, the months we've lived with this hurricane have been superior to the many years that preceded them. I'm much like those beach dwellers you see on the evening news, explaining why they won't move inland, even after being nearly swept away by some massive storm.

These people tend to stay doggedly committed to their decision to build a home three inches from the ocean, giving news cameras teary-eyed but resilient oaths that they will rebuild whatever the hurricane destroys, right after the storm has wandered off to mildly annoy people who bowed to common sense and built homes a few miles from shore

To those on the outside, it simply doesn't make sense.

"But that hurricane is destroying everything," notes the intelligent observer. "Why put yourself through that?"

The answer is that there is a difference between pleasure and happiness. Pleasure is a fleeting feeling, like the rush you get from a mouthful of sugar. My life used to be full of it.

Happiness is something else. Something so expansive and confident in its strength that it can warmly embrace things like pain, panic, chaos, sleep deprivation and even hushed voices during football games.

This happiness encompasses everything inside of it, providing a home for a wide spectrum of emotions.

A book of pithy jokes might make you chuckle for a moment, but the novels that give you the most are the same ones that make you cry, or drive you to slam them down from time to time as you grow furious at the injustices described within them.

As a dedicated hedonist for the first 35 years of my life, I know firsthand that there is more to life than enjoying oneself. And that being overly comfortable can allow a certain dullness to creep into your existence.

Call me deranged. I certainly won't blame you for it. But I like living here. In fact, I think life lived away from the wild howl of a hurricane sounds a bit boring.

THE SAGAS

There was a thick crust of snow on the ground on the night I first arrived in Mount Horeb, Wisconsin. It wasn't blanketing the earth, even in the loosest proverbial sense. These were the kinds of icy sheets that strand arctic explorers' ships, forcing them to traverse the frozen tundra on foot and eventually resort to cannibalism.

The harsh, cold, silent blue-and-white scene made the village's shops and homes look like 13th-century warships slumbering through the winter. As if they were waiting for a thaw so they could open their sails, pull up anchor and head out to pillage surrounding municipalities.

I've lived in many states and traveled to many more. Most are identical, being as they are essentially long lines of strip malls populated by chain restaurants and interspersed by residential subdivisions.

This was not. Mount Horeb, I could tell from the start, was different. It was intriguing.

It was also difficult to fully understand this little ode to Scandinavia dropped into the American Midwest.

Even the word "Scandinavian" is hard to get a handle on. It is little more than a term of convenience, referring not to any political grouping or race but generally to Denmark, Norway, Sweden, Finland and sometimes Iceland. (Like the letter "Y" in the alphabet, Iceland is wary of being steadfastly affiliated with any category or group.)

Scandinavians are a bundle of seemingly contradictory traits. For example, they conquered a large portion of the world with little more than wooden boats and iron swords, yet even today they can't pronounce the letter "J."

"What type of people cover their town with troll statues?" I wondered. *"Who buys all these Scandinavian goods?"*

I know my dad buys them. Bright sweaters on which reindeer dance and ornate silver buttons dangle, for instance. But my dad also has worn high-top shoes that are secured with slabs of Velcro for much of his adult life, so his fashion sense is dubious at best.

He thinks Velcro is one of the most astonishing technological advancements of the 20th century. He's not sure why, in sharp contrast to other major milestones like the wheel, agriculture, moveable type and computers, it failed to ever gain widespread public acceptance. The way he sees it, everyone in the world—everyone except toddlers and the elderly, that is—is wasting the vast majority of their free time tying and untying footwear. I've caught him glancing with pity at people stopped on the sidewalk to retie a lace that slipped free. To him, their stubborn adherence to outmoded technology seems almost Amish.

Still, his penchant for Scandinavian sweaters I could understand. It's cold here, and it's just as cold in Scandinavia. I once read that part of the reason Christianity was so popular when it reached Scandinavia was that Hell, with all its roaring fires, seemed almost like a tropical paradise when compared to Nifleim, the frozen Abyss of Emptiness in the north that served as the frigid afterlife destination in Norse mythology.

"For them, the searing heat of the Christian Hell was the lesser of two evils," wrote historian Magnus Magnusson, "and the real enemy was the cold that froze the sinews and paralyzed the will."

If I lived in a place so cold that it drove theological speculation in such a trajectory, I suppose I too might end up wearing some garish sweaters. I also think it's interesting that people always seem to pick a climate not unlike their own when they are trying to describe hell.

Still curious, I went to one of the shops in town that sells Scandinavian books—it didn't take long to find one— and picked up a couple anthologies containing Icelandic sagas. They are a group of stories primarily from the 13th century. People who lived in either the time or place where the tales take place didn't write them, but that slight hiccup never prevented me from reading other books, so I read one story after another until I started to understand the roots of Scandinavian culture.

I've never seen so many consonants strung together. There are people like Hrafnkel and Thjostarsson, and the characters are always going to places with names like "Svidning." Their nouns were often just the sounds chain smokers make in the early morning.

One surprising shred of information is just how many of the stories are about litigation. It's like a John Grisham novel, except every couple pages one of the characters is hacked to bits with an axe for trying to steal a horse or hunt in someone else's forest.

My favorite story is called "Thorstein the Staff-Struck." This particular tale is about several characters. They are named, not at all confusingly, Thorhall, Thorvald, Thorarin and Thorstein.

Thorarin, a former Viking, had "little money but a good many weapons," which begs the question why he didn't just sell some of his weapons. It also mentions that he was fairly "hard to deal with," which might not be the first time that phrase was applied to a Viking.

The narrative is proof that Westerns are tame compared to Icelandic sagas. In John Wayne movies, people ride on horses and occasionally fight with other cowboys. In "Thorstein the Staff-Struck," they make the horses fight each other. Shockingly, the organized horse fight doesn't end well. Basically, the horses kick and bite each other, which was socially acceptable, but then a man hits a horse, which apparently was not, so another man hits the other horse. Then the first man hits the second man, things get out of hand and spectators who paid to see two horses kick each other get to watch a couple of bonus fights for free.

Throughout the rest of the story, people do a lot of murdering in the name of revenge. They also do a little cooking of sheep's heads, because anyone genius enough to fight horses likes to keep mentally fit by eating a lot of sheep brains. It all culminates in a long sword fight, during which occurs one of the earliest versions of the "my shoelace is untied" excuse in athletic history. (During the battle, one man calls for a timeout because his "shoe-thong" is loose.)

Come to think of it, I guess it's further proof that my dad is right about Velcro.

A CHRISTMAS STORY

My favorite professor in college had an STD.

Dr. Thompson earned his Sacred Theology Doctorate while cloistered as a Franciscan monk. He grew up in Minnesota then left for Europe, where he joined a monastery for twenty years and became an expert on Bonaventure, a 13th-century Italian saint.

Bonaventure himself had been a follower of St. Francis of Assisi, a 12th-century saint who, along with several gnomes, served as the model for most of the statues you see on sale at typical garden centers today. The patron saint of animals, St. Francis, is usually depicted in a rustic robe with several squirrels and rabbits at his feet and a flock of assorted songbirds alighting on his shoulders, as if he smelled perpetually of sunflower seeds.

After two decades, Dr. Thompson left the monastery to get reacquainted with the temporal world. He bumped into an old acquaintance—an Italian woman who had been a nun during the same period—the two fell in love and eventually married, settling in a Florida suburb near the college I attended.

Dr. Thompson did what all wise college professors do—he assigned a book he had written (on Bonaventure) as part of the required reading each semester. In doing so, he kept the tome in print. If he managed to stay in academia for several decades, the resulting sales could eventually add up and pay for an in-ground pool, he pointed out.

Dr. Thompson took erudition to vertigo-inducing heights. For starters, he appeared to be fluent in whatever language was most appropriate at any given moment.

A student who hailed from Barcelona and liked to wear black t-shirts small enough to fit snuggly on a common action figure, once scoffed at something he said during a lecture. Dr. Thompson turned sharply in his direction and unleashed a calm and quiet but apparently terrifying series of Spanish words, causing the student's olive skin to chalken.

Sometimes, when English wasn't sufficient, Dr. Thompson would remove his glasses, polishing them on the front of his shirt while saying things like: "Well, the Danes have a saying about this, but it doesn't translate well into English" or "Perhaps this conversation can only be held effectively in Manx."

His favorite, however, was to state rhetorically: "Well, you know what the Babylonians say."

The name of the culture might change—it could be the ancient Celts or the tribesmen of Papua New Guinea—but it was clear their dialect was the only way to express what he was thinking. He wasn't trying to be pretentious. It was just that the English words for many of his ideas hadn't been invented yet.

He once allowed us to attend a small gathering at his home. Upon entering, we realized he shopped for furnishings in the same place as Indiana Jones. End tables were stacked with relics, chalices and things covered in gilt. Everything was medieval, and the wine wasn't much younger.

His maps were old. Old enough to still include the USSR. Old enough to feature monsters.

He loved the Rolling Stones and Prince, and sometimes played their music in class.

I eventually stopped telling people outside of school what I was studying because it invariably led to one question.

"So you're gonna become a preacher or something?" everyone at the beachside bars said with mild surprise. "You don't seem the type."

But assuming anyone who studies religion is planning to become a priest is like thinking someone in sports medicine is training to become a knee brace, or that someone in culinary school is studying to someday find steady employment as a bowl of soup.

I started college as an English major, but the stories did not contain enough passages detailing widespread death and suffering to suit my tastes. Likewise, love was mitigated to a narrow, one-dimensional interpretation in most literature.

At the end of my first class with Dr. Thompson, I was hooked on ancient and modern theology, and I told him so.

"If good stories are what you are interested in, the religion program might be of some interest to you," he said, adding with a chuckle: "You know what the Maasai say."

I didn't, but I switched my major anyway.

Every religion held the key to a treasure trove of stories. I was reminded of this when I later interviewed a member of the Ho Chunk Nation. He explained to me that in his religion, certain stories should only be told at specified times of year.

In the European tradition, Christmas is the time when stories are most abundant. They include not just biblical tales, but those from our own childhoods as well.

The farm on which I grew up was owned by an elderly British woman who looked exactly like George Washington. She even had the same hairstyle. The only difference was that she was much taller and broad shouldered than I imagined the first president to be.

Each Christmas Eve she visited our family. She would pull up to our gravel driveway, perched atop the whirring motorized golf cart she used to zoom around the farm. She would dismount and, leaving a pack of semi-feral dogs to guard the eggshell-white plastic cart, come inside to have a glass of brandy by the tree.

The gifts weren't memorable, but Mrs. S, which is what we called the monolithic woman, always fashioned color-ful—if slightly asymmetrical—hats out of the shreds and strips of wrapping paper and ribbon lying on the ground. The hats were always a bit tipsy, not unlike Mrs. S herself come to think of it, but the routine never grew old for my sister and me.

When I was very young, my mother told me that each year, for the few minutes following the stroke of midnight on Christmas, all of the animals in the barn gained the ability to speak in perfect English. And this was Massachusetts, where most people speak in an accent that outsiders can only mimic by eating several hot peppers, then subjecting themselves to a series of blows to the head. The idea that livestock had figured out how to clearly articulate ideas before the humans had intrigued me.

In the weeks leading up to Christmas, I dreamed of staying up late and visiting the heavy horse barn, where I could finally learn why the animals were so eager to kick or otherwise maim me. Then we could all partake in my favorite form of language as a child: swearing.

I always fell asleep too early, and therefore never found out, but to this day I still have the urge to poke my head into the nearest barn on Christmas Eve.

One year, when I was still very small in both stature and intellectual prowess, a portion of one of my presents, being slender in shape, mysteriously broke free from its wrapping. Uncloaked, the tip of the present looked like only one thing to my young eyes: a wizard's wand.

I had recently watched a movie that brought the existence of magical wands to my attention. Unfortunately, the film failed to explain that such items do not technically exist in the real world.

I considered ripping the remaining paper off; perhaps the wand was like food and had to be used within a certain abbreviated timeframe after the seal had been broken or else its powers would spoil or rot. Plus, I reasoned, if my hunch was correct, I could probably play with the wand for several days, then turn back time and place it back in the package without my parents ever knowing.

I chose to wait for my prize and spent the days leading up until Christmas vividly imagining the time, place and manner of the torture I would inflict on my many oppressors once I had harnessed mystical powers.

But the stem protruding through the wrapping paper was actually the antenna component of one of two walkie-talkies my parents had purchased for me.

My personality ran toward stubborn as a child, and my parents looked at me with discernible surprise when I quickly got to work using my new gift to cast imaginary spells on anything that walked by.

Even at a young age I was aware that St. Nicholas' "good" and "bad" dichotomy had to be, on some level, subjective. If I used my wand to travel back in time and kill Hitler when he was still a baby, thereby preventing millions of deaths, would Santa withhold my presents because I had committed a "bad" act?

Or would he look at the circumstances surrounding my deeds and their ultimate impact on society as a whole when passing judgment?

Adults acted as if I were trying to provoke them when I made inquiries on the matter. "Just stop painting on the walls, clean up your room and he'll give you presents, okay?" my mother said when I asked her Santa's political views.

It remained unclear whether Santa's moral judgment leaned toward Kantian or utilitarian. On the other hand, I was certain his information-gathering network contained gaping holes. Every year, I committed various deeds that were unquestionably bad, but every year I received a pile of gifts, the size and nature of which seemingly had no correlation to my behavior.

Except for one year.

My swearing and wall painting must have been particularly egregious that year, because someone placed real coal in my stocking. I had heard from my parents that bad children received this inordinately heavy and messy rock in their stockings, but no classmates at school had ever reported getting any, and I knew some of them were worse than I was. I had never even tortured any animal that had fur—a claim several classmates could never make with a straight face.

So it came as a shock when I reached into my stocking and withdrew a hand covered in soot and grime, then dumped out a pile of coal onto the floor. A few minutes later, I received my real presents, but the coal was either a warning or a practical joke. It disturbed me that this elderly man, who had a definite but arcane connection to Jesus, would go out of his way to make me cry, but the point was clear.

For the most part, however, Santa was kind. I always baked cookies with my mother, leaving them stacked on a plate next to a glass of fresh milk before I trampled up the stairs to bed. I left fresh carrots for the reindeer. Alongside the edible bribe, I placed a note thanking Santa in advance, even if I received only very small presents or none at all.

"If you want to just give everyone peace on earth, or feed the starving children in Ethiopia instead of bringing me a Batmobile, that would be fine with me too," I wrote, gritting my teeth. The goal, of course, was to sway his judgment about my moral character, which would in turn lead to more presents under my tree.

One Christmas Eve, I accompanied the family of a school friend to Mass at their church. Once I took my place on the rigid wooden seat, I made a pleasing discovery. Apparently aware of my short attention span and the protracted nature of the ensuing religious ceremony, a member of the clergy had thoughtfully placed a red candle in a slot on the back of the pew in front of me.

If warmed in a human hand, such wax becomes pliable and can be molded into any number of interesting shapes, so I got to work creating small, heavily-armed action figures.

My friend's mother made animated gestures in my direction, but their meaning was obscure so I continued. About twenty minutes into the service, however, someone else sent a clearer message when a man sitting a few rows behind us had a heart attack and had to be carted out of the hushed church by paramedics. It occurred to me that the metaphysical lightning bolt might have been intended for me and simply missed by a couple yards. I knew Santa and God shared some sort of connection—perhaps Santa used fossil fuels to warn children and God used heart attacks.

So, just as I heard a voice say something about the Prince of Peace, I placed my drippy red soldiers on top of the hymnal and focused my attention on the proceedings.

The difficulty came when, at the end of the service, everyone lit their candles and marched down the aisles in single file. Anyone close enough, or anyone with a decent overhead view and superhuman vision, for that matter, would have noticed that my candle was different—it was the only one in the shape of Arnold Schwarzenegger's character in the movie *Predator.*

Because my parents were products of the 1960s, they set out to raise me according to a set of ideals that coincided with their own pacifistic views. One rule was simple: no toy weapons.

This meant that no matter how many times I asked for toy guns at Christmas, I was disappointed. Today, with a few more years under his belt and me not incarcerated, my father has adopted a slightly modified view of this philosophy.

"You spent all of your time making weapons," he says thoughtfully. "Guns with blocks of wood and rubber bands, bows and arrows; everything sharp ended up turned into a sword."

To compound the problem, we lived on a farm where the spare parts needed to fashion real weaponry were readily available. I was prohibited from owning a plastic cap gun, but whenever I felt the inclination, I could wander into the workshop adjacent to the barn and use a variety of power tools capable of slicing through a human femur as if it were tepid butter.

The result was an impressive arsenal that was constantly being confiscated and a set of scars I'm pretty sure I will keep until decomposition sets in.

Another by-product of an agricultural upbringing was that Santa's notes were always written in the tone of a farmer. For someone who lived forever and could fly, he seemed overly worried about various problems with the livestock. The notes almost sounded like they had been written by my father.

"Merry Christmas, Matthew," the message said one year. "Prancer's hoof is giving her trouble after a recent bout of thrush, and Dancer got his neck stuck in a fence the other day. Plus, the price of hay has just skyrocketed recently thanks to the Senate's inept handling of the Farm Bill. P.S. Stop making guns out of your father's tools."

People often make snarky comments about the consumerist nature of Christmas in America, and they like to suggest anyone sentimental about it is either a religious zealot or someone desperately trying to sell you something.

But the reason I get a warm, fuzzy feeling is that this is the time of year when I remember all of these stories, and stories are, well...

You know what the Aborigines of western Australia say.

LIFE AND DEATH
AT THE ZOO

We probably looked odd through the glowing yellow windows as we rode home from work on the train.

Me, my khaki pants streaked with horse manure and camel dung. My purple, short-sleeved, collared shirt coated with an earthy *papier mâché* of dust and sweat.

And the business people, their suits just barely wrinkled from days spent telling soft lies on cell phones, the faint odor of fatty, salty chain restaurant food emanating from their fabric.

They always bunched together, like some herd of grassland herbivores, hoping my eyes would be confused by the way their cheap suits blended together as they stood clustered around a watering hole. Only they were gathered around an emergency exit.

I knew they were jealous because I carried with me stories more valuable than anything they bought or sold that day. No one who smelled the way I did could possibly be without a good narrative.

My favorite was about Robbie.

Robbie was an elderly Clydesdale. I worked at a major metropolitan zoo, giving horse and camel rides to paying customers and caring for the animals while we weren't walking in circles on a gravel track.

Todd, my boss, compensated for his diminutive height and dearth of chin by speaking in an extremely loud voice. He had owned a pet mountain lion as a kid, growing up in rural Indiana. He told me he used to walk it on a leash. When he was 13, he saved up his allowance and purchased a pet Capuchin monkey.

"And what is he going to do?" his mother asked, staring at the pair of little primates.

Looking straight up at her with a steadfast gaze, my future boss responded: "He's going to be my friend."

"He knew he had to wear a diaper," Todd recalled in a shout, slapping his little knee with a hand that looked like it had been amputated from someone much larger and surgically attached to his wrist, "so he'd hop up on the table and lie down with his legs up in the air. It was his way of saying: 'Let's get his show on the road!'"

About two dozen of us worked at the zoo that summer. Most were from the economically blighted neighborhoods that surrounded the zoo.

There was also another Matt. With freckles the size of raisins, round spectacles, and a receding red hairline—all at the tender age of 23. His prior job had been with a traveling circus.

Then there was Martha. She had a voice like a lawnmower and complained constantly of phantom ailments. She wore knee braces and wrapped her wrists in protective gauze. She owned a pet rattlesnake and a bloodhound puppy.

My best friend at the zoo was James. He had the facial features and girth of Shrek if you painted him the color of a dark-roast coffee bean. He stood six feet five inches tall and weighed close to 350 pounds, thanks to a steady diet of zoo hot dogs. His unexpected soprano rang out from something deep and seismic within his formidable gut.

The zoo job paid minimum wage and there were no days off, because animals need to eat whether kids have ridden around on them that day or not. Children whose exposure to wildlife had previously been limited to pit bulls, pigeons and a few rodents came to see what else the planet had to offer. To see creatures from every corner of a globe most would never have the means to explore.

As common as he was next to a red panda or sloth bear, Robbie the horse inspired rapt awe in every visitor. He was in an advanced state of decay, but his ruddy coat and the long, white tufts of hair around his feet made people stop and stare.

One morning, we arrived to find him dying on the floor of the barn. He wasn't shaking because he was scared, or because of the chill that conspired with his wetness. He shook because his front legs couldn't support all the weight. His rump was deep in a hole and his hind leg on the far side had disappeared somewhere beneath him.

His chest was still up, with his legs splayed out in front of him. He looked like a dog. A two-thousand-pound, dark, sopping wet creature expiring because he no longer had the strength to support his size.

I grasped the lead under his pink heaving nostrils and leaned back. He groaned and only managed to push a little more sand up around him. His breathing was hard and regular on my face, and it hit me every few seconds like the air from a balmy, depressing fan set to oscillate.

We only worked him for an hour each morning, sometimes less. Just enough to make it seem like he was still useful. Todd had purchased him for $50 at an auction, saving him from a grim fate.

No matter how much we fed him, his hips always stuck out at a funny angle. The darkest hair on his neck was light gray and brittle. He could take off his own saddle by breathing out all his air and rubbing the leather girth strap on a fence post.

We made up an old-man voice for him and said things in it all day to pass the time—saying what he would have but couldn't. Everything was advice and started with "You know son…" or "In my day…".

Sometimes we told kids that Robbie had worked for Budweiser as a young gelding. "He used to pull that big beer cart," we would say. "He was the lead horse." Robbie's eyes seemed to glint when we told the tall tales and massaged his neck.

One morning, we noticed Robbie had some kind of skin infection in his most private of areas. The boss gave him antibiotics and told me to hold a warm compress on it three times a day. Every day for two weeks, I held a wet cloth there in front of giggling schoolchildren and many more giggling adults. I wondered if some day the zoo would put up one of its informational signs outside the pen. "In this enclosure, you will see a man with a bachelor's degree in philosophy holding a wet cloth on an elderly horse's penis."

The other horses, who were younger and jet black in color, tried to kick Robbie, so we tied him off by himself under the trees. He would slowly chew on hay with his dull, short, beige teeth, leaning on a post and trying to take off his saddle when no one was looking.

I thought maybe his life had been more fantastic than anything we made up for the children. He had scars on his sides and most of his teeth were cracked. When we would sit, after work, on the dusty hay bales next to him, he would pull his head up from his grain every few minutes and the molasses-soaked pellets would dribble from his mouth while he listened to something we could not hear. Perhaps the echo of some memory.

On the day he died, we pulled Robbie away from the wall a few inches and propped him up with a stack of hay bails. Martha covered him with cotton blankets. The one draped over his neck was pink with rotund little Care Bears on it. All the strength had gone out of him.

When I was a little kid, my parents used to take me to a grungy little pizza place in a neighborhood founded by Greek fishermen and their descendants. On the wall above the corner booth where we always sat was a small plastic statue of a team of Clydesdales pulling a red beer cart. I always begged my dad to buy it for me. That was twenty years earlier when Robbie was probably young and healthy, wherever he was and whatever he was doing. Certainly not old and dying on a barn floor.

Martha kept crying. Robbie looked curiously at her, probably wondering why she was so upset at the end of another ordinary day.

When he was gone, we poured big splashes of our evening beer into the dirt, toasting a life we knew very little about but genuinely missed. We spent the next several hours making up stories, giving Robbie's life one noble context after another.

"Someday," James told me as we sat together in our collared, purple zoo shirts and dung-stained khaki pants, "you should write a story about him."

WHEN NO ONE IS WATCHING

I don't dance. Even more importantly, other people, primarily those with eyeballs, don't want me to.

I don't remember exactly when this decision was made. I know I danced freely around my parents' kitchen as a child. Then, on a day I don't specifically remember, I tried to dance in public.

That would have been the moment I looked around and realized I had never really been dancing at all. Other people were dancing to the rhythm of the music. I had only been moving around while music played. These two things—the music and I—were two unrelated occurrences happening simultaneously. Merging the reality of the music with the reality of my frame required alchemy beyond my humble powers.

So I resigned myself to spectating. It wasn't so bad, really.

I had other friends whose abilities were no better than my own. But for reasons I never understood, they danced on. Even though they tended to look like they were trying to mount a lubricated ostrich.

Sometimes I do envy them.

Throughout our lives, most motion is simply a means to an end. You walk to the store. You drive to work. You run away from the person who wants to chat about the cute things their cats do.

The dance floor is one of the only places where movement exists for its own sake. One of the only times in your life you have arrived at your destination and you don't have to immediately set off for a new waypoint.

When bad dancers start moving, they tend to fall into two categories. Most simply make a short, visual announcement to the world that they are very bad at procreation. Others stride defiantly into the crowd, move a foot or a finger, remember they can't dance, then try to act as if the dance floor is an un-circumventable area on their way to some other destination.

Those who are too mired in jerky gyrations sometimes adopt an expression intended to suggest they have only recently returned from an out-of-body experience, or perhaps were sleep-walking and woke up to find themselves surrounded by swaying bodies and loud music.

It's simply too late for me. If I started dancing now it would be too jarring for my family and friends. The way I'd feel if my dog started asking me how I felt about a carbon tax, in French.

I don't refuse to dance because I'm embarrassed. I don't dance because I'm a nice guy and I don't want to needlessly upset people.

Parties are places where pleasant things happen, and it would be cruel for me to introduce some unpleasantness.

Even if I were friends with a person who was blind, I wouldn't risk it. "That sounds," I imagine them saying, "awful."

And if I worked really hard and became a great dancer, people would be suspicious. "What else has he been hiding from us?" they would wonder.

Until recently, "dance partner" was synonymous with "victim" in my vocabulary. The closest I came to pulling it off was during barn dances, where if I had a long-enough beard and a red-enough flannel shirt, I looked vaguely like I was supposed to be there.

Then everything changed.

Now, for the first time, I have a willing dance partner. In between diaper changes and bottles of milk, my little daughter demands to be danced. She doesn't care about the song, or whether or not I look like a wounded animal when I do it.

And she can't speak English yet, so I'm free to imagine what she's thinking. It's usually something along the lines of: "Those are some great moves, dad."

There is a saying that we should all "dance like no one is watching," but when she gets old enough to dance on her own two feet, she'll probably ask why I don't dance at parties.

"I dance," I'll say with a wink, "*when* no one is watching."

TWO MASKED MEN

From the ages of six to 12, I dressed as Batman. When not wearing a cape, I went around as a young Bruce Wayne. I was only Matt Geiger when I had to go to school, or when Bruce had to go undercover for a special mission.

Around the same time, people made a lot of movies on the farm where I lived. The on-camera stuff varied, with a few commercials thrown in, but each shoot was similar. A glob of people in ill-fitting leather, with grease in their hair and perfumes that floated around them like synthetic, unpleasant auras.

Organic beings, from the smallest leghorn chick to the largest Holstein bull, have a certain lightness of bearing. A smoothness of movement indicative that they are traveling through the world according to certain immutable laws. They are swimming with the current of life.

These film crews defied those laws. Their anti-functional clothing creaked as they strutted awkwardly across the barnyard. They worked feverishly to block out the actual sunlight and recreate a more "realistic" lighting effect for their easily befuddled cameras.

"Hey there, little guy!" some woman, lacquered in makeup and tottering on high heels not designed for gravel or cow manure, would squeal as I came around the corner of the shed. "Did you get all dressed up for us today?"

"*Oh*," I thought to myself, flapping my cape for dramatic effect and struggling, as I always did, to see out of my mask's elusive eyeholes. "*Looks like they're shooting some kind of commercial here today.*"

Then aloud to the woman: "Of course! I got dressed up just for you!"

Something about my costumes, for I had several iterations on the Batman theme, which I selected depending on mood and weather, reminded these jaded, forlorn people of something once important to them. It was, I know now, the reason most of them had gotten involved in their particular industry.

At one point they had been organic beings, wearing tights and clambering with ease over rooftops, their table-cloth capes billowing behind them as they loped along. One day, when a real-life adult or classmate replaced their imaginary villains, informing them they were suddenly too old to play make-believe, they had scrambled to find some loophole. Some way they could carry on this joyous charade.

"I've got it," they'd realize, gazing down at a too-small costume they'd been forbidden to wear in middle school. "I'll go into show business."

Years later, they found themselves on a vast farm, looking like extras on some cop drama set in New York. Sipping bad coffee from soggy paper cups and holding various clipboards, they destroyed various settings in order to recreate fake ones that looked, to them and their gullible cameras, more realistic.

When they saw a little farm boy throwing a homemade grappling hook around the chimney atop his parents' house, his eyes flashing with a joy that was borderline deranged on those rare moments when the mask's eyeholes happened to pass over them, something inside those film crews snorted, shifted, and gradually began to awaken from its slumber.

"So you like Batman, huh?" they would inevitably ask me.

And I did.

I had friends who worshiped other superheroes. Some liked Superman. Others, Spiderman. Still others liked the endless parade of X-Men, who frequently died and came back to life wearing ever more gaudy colors.

I stuck with Batman. I enjoyed the fact that he had no superpowers. (*"Just like me!"* I thought to myself.) Plus, the fact that his exorbitant wealth could not transcend the pain of his slain family made him seem so much more melancholy, and therefore more real, than the comic book characters who flew around with big grins on their faces and lasers shooting out of their eyes.

I didn't know anyone who had been bitten by a radioactive spider, and I didn't know anyone who had been born bulletproof, on another planet, and jettisoned here. But I did know death and loss.

We were all mortal, and those around us would all inevitably die, I thought to myself. We were all just like Batman.

It was a sad thought that made me very, very happy.

And while Bruce Wayne was incredibly wealthy, I knew rich people did exist, even if I only knew it in the way that I know grizzly bears and jaguars roam the earth. They definitely inhabit the world, but they are rarely, if ever, spotted hanging around my house.

Seeing hundreds of people, all but a select few carrying equipment, descend on a vacant field filled me with expectation. I would soon be reminded, however, that filming—be it for TV or the movies—is the most boring activity known to man.

By noon, I would have abandoned them to go about my business, scaling rooftops and looking for calves and barn cats to save from super villains in my own, decidedly rural version of Gotham City.

Little things stuck with me. The supermarket set that included entirely plastic "fresh produce." An actor who was wearing overalls and playing a farmer, and was so deathly afraid of cows he whimpered and fled when they meandered in his general direction.

The time they filmed part of the Academy-Award-winning Civil War film *Glory*, transformed one of our pastures into a bloody, corpse-littered battlefield.

The *Karate Kid* movie scene they filmed inside one of our hay barns. Whenever I see that movie on late night TV, even to this day, all I can think is, "There are literally hundreds of raccoon droppings on the floor."

And the time I got to meet Cary Elwes, who played the "Dread Pirate Roberts" in the 1987 film, *The Princess Bride.*

I'm still happy to report that he was genuinely nice to a random farm kid who ran up to him and asked for an autograph. We shared a nice moment, the two of us, just a sliver of time between two masked men.

THREE SHOTS

There is a story about a little boy, a shotgun, and death.

The child goes on a fishing trip with his father in Upper Michigan. One night, the boy's father heads out onto the dark, still water of a nearby lake to fish by jacklight. Before he leaves the tent, he hands a loaded firearm to his son.

He tells the child to fire three shots if he faces danger or grows afraid.

After his father leaves, the boy lies alone in the tent, gazing blindly into the void of darkness that swallows anyone who ventures into the night after the sun has made its retreat.

He hears animals crying out. Then, for the first time in his life, he realizes with cold horror that someday he will die. That he must die.

It is a hard, immutable, uncaring fact.

Out on the lake, his father hears three gunshots ring out and then fade away into dreadful silence.

Rushing back, he finds his son sound asleep in the tent. He will die someday, but not tonight. And by firing those shots into the dark void, like the hooting owl or the barking fox, he has given voice to his fear and broken the paralysis that the specter of death can produce in its future victims.

Death cannot ever be defeated, but it can be beaten back by those who cry out. By those who fire their three shots when the darkness and the stillness are more than their souls can bear.

These are the types of things you think about when you are sitting in the emergency room—that emporium of hand sanitizer and human misery—with your toddler in the middle of the night.

"This is a narcotic, okay?" asked the nurse, yanking me away from my grim train of thought.

"Great!" I responded, looking at the small, plastic device that was about to shoot medication up my little girl's nose.

It was a marked departure from my prior parenting philosophy. I was, in that moment, a new man. There had been a Matt Geiger who lived in my house, wore my clothes and drove my car. He planned to raise his daughter on the feeling of sunshine, the pleasant aroma of sunflowers, and positive sentiments. To treat her injuries with classical music and passages read from *Anna Karenina*.

In that moment, in the emergency room, I, the new me, thought back on that man as a loveable, naïve oaf. As a person who had a really great beard, sure, but who had little or no concept of the outside world.

It had been a long night. Far longer than the printout we received when our little girl was discharged from the hospital the following morning. That sheet of paper suggests that she had been suffering from a brief viral infection that caused excruciating pain in her hip joint, and an accompanying fever that had broken by the time the sun rose.

This is a significantly less dramatic presentation of the situation than my initial, fatherly diagnosis, which was "Legs falling off! Head on fire!"

The waiting room of an emergency room is an excellent place to regain perspective.

On our special night, we were surrounded by an assortment of maladies. Heart palpitations. An overdose. A suicide attempt. A woman whose forehead looked like it had collided with a brick, a woman whose facial expression suggested she had been having a really great time until the exact moment the brick arrived. A string of people being ushered in for blood alcohol and drug testing.

And my little girl, whose condition was surprisingly resilient when treated by saying: "There, there—there, there…" over and over again.

When we had woken up that morning, none of us had had any intention of ending our day in this place, surrounded by blue smocks and wall murals so forcefully cheerful they made it painfully clear that this was a building where terrible things happen on a routine basis.

When my daughter lost the ability to walk, crawl, or even sit up later that morning, I was content to turn her into a miniature Hunter S. Thompson. I would have been happy to put a white bucket hat on her sweaty little forehead and a neon tropical shirt on her splotchy torso. Just as long as we could get her some drugs. *Bring on the drugs*, I thought.

A few moments after receiving the narcotic, she forgot all about her leg pain. Sitting up in her institutional white hospital bed, she began appreciating music on a whole new level. Swinging her head around at me, she smiled dreamily and began bobbing her head to an insurance jingle that was floating down from a wall-mounted television.

With the panic receding, I took a moment to reflect on where we were.

It had been an evening of confusion, which for me is nothing new. For instance, the part of my brain that understands the difference between a podiatrist (a foot doctor) and a pediatrician (a children's doctor) has been broken for quite some time. So when the ER doctors briefly mentioned calling in a pediatric surgeon to examine her hip, I nearly cried out: "No, her feet are fine!"

There was also broader confusion. Why were nature and luck being so mean to my kid, and by extension to me?

The next morning, as the sun rose and chased away our terror, her symptoms vanished. She was fine, and we headed home to a blissfully normal morning in our wonderfully mundane little house in our beautifully banal small town in Wisconsin.

She is fine, and I'm fine, and most of the people we know are all fine. For today, at least.

The author of *Three Shots*, Ernest Hemingway, eventually ended his own life with a single, literal shot. I sometimes wish he had found the strength to fire a few metaphysical shots instead, perhaps crying out by penning one more story to help fend off the fear. But in the end, one shot, from a shotgun, was all it took to make sure he would never have to feel dread again.

But for those who fear death, and even those who will eventually be overrun by the fear of it and flee silently into its eternal embrace, the best way to spend our remaining days is to fire our three figurative shots. To create paintings, novels, songs, really good cakes and even silly little stories about the time we had to take our daughter to the emergency room. Because once we fire them, we can always sleep a little better until the sun returns.

ABOUT THE AUTHOR

Matt Geiger was born in Brunswick, Maine, in 1979 and grew up at Appleton Farms in Ipswich, Massachusetts. He studied philosophy and religion at Flagler College and went on to write for newspapers and magazines in Florida, Wisconsin, and the United Kingdom. His work has won various journalism awards, including four from the Wisconsin Newspaper Association for the stories in this book.

He currently lives in Wisconsin with his wife, his daughter, two dogs, a cat, and a flock of chickens.

You can contact Matt through his website
www.geigerbooks.com

CPSIA information can be obtained
at www.ICGtesting.com
Printed in the USA
FFOW04n1716271116
29754FF